To George
Kindred Spirit
Bob Clark
December 9, 2008

Stories Carved In Stone
Westfield Massachusetts

by Bob Clark

Photographs by the Author

2008
Published by
Dog Pond Press, P.O. Box 27, West Springfield, Massachusetts 01090

For Rusty
All ways

ISBN 978-0-9755362-3-0
Library of Congress Control Number: 2008906447

FIRST PRINTING

Cover design by Rusty Clark

Introduction

"Stories Carved in Stone" is a perfectly apt title for this wonderful series by Rusty and Bob Clark. Since it opened in 1868, the Westfield Athenaeum has been serving the needs of the greater Westfield, Massachusetts, community in part by collecting, identifying and preserving historical documents and artifacts for future generations. We cannot know exactly what information will be important to future historians, but we surely recognize the importance of local cemeteries and the need to collect and organize the information that can be gleaned from cemetery records, gravestones and monuments to those who came before us. Walk into any burying ground on a crisp November day in New England and read the inscriptions carved on the old stones. Some stones may be barely readable and others may be fallen over, with pieces broken and words missing. No matter the state of the stones, there is a story behind every inscription and the stones speak to us, if we take the time to look and listen. Thankfully, this wonderful series of books has made our work easier by capturing these important stories before they disappear and by preserving them for posterity.

Westfield has its share of famous and not-so-famous people, many lying in close proximity to each other in hallowed burying grounds that go back centuries. Many of the oldest stones can be found in the Mechanic Street Cemetery, known as the Old Burying Ground, where the oldest stone is dated 1683 (Westfield was established in 1669), or in a private cemetery known as Pine Hill Cemetery. Just eighteen stones can be found in the Mundale Cemetery, located in the woods shaded by large pine trees. There are also cemeteries connected with local churches, such as St. Mary

Cemetery, St. John Lutheran Church Cemetery, and St. Joseph Polish National Catholic Church Cemetery. Part of our communal history is written on the gravestones, some telling of Westfield's role in the Revolutionary War, or more recently in World War I and World War II, while others tell of epidemics, floods, drownings, industrial accidents, homicides, fires and other misfortunes. Some graves are unmarked, leaving us to guess at what befell those who are buried there.

If you find yourself wandering in one of Westfield's graveyards one day and you come upon a stone that says "Hannah, Relict of Paul Noble," you will have found someone who lived to the ripe old age of 100. How did she live to such an age without the benefit of modern medicine? Surely, there is a story there. Let us take the time to learn about those who, like Hannah, lived and died long before we were born; let us take time to learn their names and their children's names, and let us take time to honor them. Whether the people whose names you read lived for one year or one hundred, they have a story to tell and they deserve to be remembered.

Chris Lindquist
Director, Westfield Athenaeum

Table of Contents

The Wild, Wild West

Fear and trepidation abounded in the countryside. By daylight, men folk tended the fields and built homes and outbuildings with loaded weapons always within reach, while the women folk did the household chores and raised the young children. At dusk everyone hurried inside the fort and locked the gates, which were to remain unopened until dawn the next day. Anyone caught outside was left to fend for themselves--no exceptions. The entire town huddled at night, sleeping together for safety. All of the town houses were built inside the fort, another two square miles of property was fenced around it. Wild and savage Indians were waiting outside the fort to take the scalps and the lives of the people they could find, and the townsfolk were taking no chances.

This was the wild, wild west. If you close your eyes for a minute, are you picturing cowboys and Indians in the American Midwest of the 1870s? It wasn't *that* wild, wild west. This was over two hundred years earlier, in the wilds of western Massachusetts. It took hardy and brave pioneers to settle here. When the Westfield area was settled in the mid 1660s, it was the westernmost frontier town in the Massachusetts Bay Colony, and retained that distinction until 1725. Strict rules of conduct and dress existed in Westfield during the early years, " . . . it [is] considered contrary to honest and sober order and Demeanor, not becoming a wilderness state; at Least ye

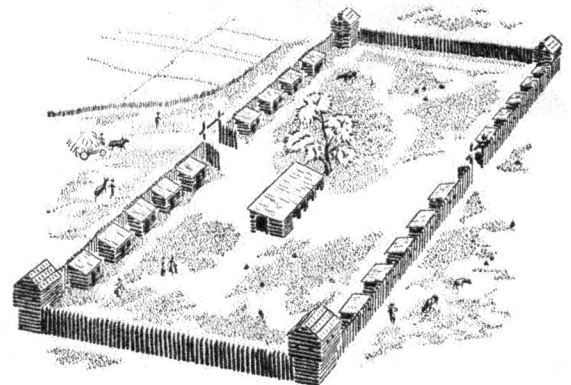

Profession of Christianity and Religion to wear silk in a flaunting manner and long hair and other extravagances beyond ones means or station, and we find Hugh Dudley and wife, Elizabeth Cooke and Mary Fowler of Westfield before the Court for disobeying this law." In January of 1675 there were witchcraft trials held in Northampton, just to the north, in an attempt to solidify the religious community.

The upper Connecticut River valley was settled not for religious reasons, like the initial Puritan settlers to the east, but for commercial reasons. The area was bountiful in beaver, one of the prime exportable resources being sold to England. Beaver hats and accessories were all the rage in Europe, and the beaver had been hunted to near extinction there, making the pelts collected here extremely valuable. Three traders set up a trading post on Westfield's Little River around 1640, staying there for at least a year and a half before disappearing without a trace. It is assumed that they were either carried off, or killed outright, by the local natives. This was such a fertile area that both Massachusetts and Connecticut laid claim to it. When Westfield was officially incorporated as a town in 1669, more than half of the population originally hailed from Connecticut.

Wolves were abundant in the Westfield area, causing problems with crops and livestock. In an effort to control the population, a bounty of ten shillings a head was placed on each wolf pelt, creating a steady source of income for some of the local hunters. One story is told of an elderly Indian who regularly brought in pelts. When a local hunter was visiting, trying to find out the Indian's secret, an old she-wolf walked by. When asked why he didn't kill her, the Indian replied, "Me have no more young ones then."

Thomas Cooper, from Springfield, was awarded a land grant of almost three hundred sixty acres in Woronoco, one of the early names given to the Westfield area, on December 4, 1658. The first settlers, Joseph Sackett, Walter Lee, and George Saxton, arrived in 1663. At a town meeting in Springfield on February 7, 1665, a committee consisting of Captain John Pynchon, Major Eleazur Holyoke, Nathaniel Ely, George Colton, and Benjamin Cooley, was chosen to oversee the settling of Westfield, making land grants in that territory. In July of 1666, lots between twenty and fifty acres were granted to Captain Aaron Cook, James Cornish, Thomas Dewey, John Ingersol, Joseph Leeds, Moses Cook, John Osborn, Major John Holyoke, David Ashley, Thomas Noble, Sergeant Thomas Stebbins, Samuel Marshfield, John Ponder, John Root, Hugh Dudley, William Brooke, Thomas Orton, and Benjamin Cooley, "which Thomas Gun hath by exchange for land on the northerly side (the river) 14 acres." On March 12, 1667, "the inhabitants of Waranoco spetially those that live at the Cellars judging it necessary that there should be a highway across the wet meadow under the hill for their passage to the pyne plains. The Committee doe determine order & appoint George Phelps & John Williams to lay out a high way where it is most convenient for

the end aforesaid. And it is determined that if John Sackett's five acres across over the brooke doe come within the common fence that then he shall fence for it." At a General Court of Election held at Boston, May 19, 1669, "there being a motion made to this court in behalf of the inhabitants at Woronoke, belonging to Springfield, that they may be a township of themselves, Springfield being willing . . . that the said towne be called Westfield."

In a court decision between the Indians and Lieutenant Thomas Cooper, "the land wch the Indians thus challenged, they did engage before the Corte that it shall be secure to him, the said Lieut. Cooper, which land is bounded northerly by the hill that stretches down to John Sackets, westerly the hill Wasapacatuck, southerly by Worronoke River, easterly by a strait lyne drawen northerly from ye mouth of the little river calling the Fort River, to the graves and from ye graves still northerly to ye sd hill yt goes down to John Sackett's, fromward the other hill called Wasapacatuck. Confirmed by the Corte 26 Sept., 1671."

Joseph Whitney and David Ashley were awarded a grant on March 19, 1668, to build a grist mill on Sackett's Creek. While that venture failed, a mill built in 1672, owned by Joseph Whiting and the Dewey brothers, Thomas, Josiah, and Jedediah, on Two Mile Creek in the Little River district thrived. When John Pynchon's mill was burned by the Indians in King Philip's War, the people of Springfield were forced to use the mill in Westfield, despite having to travel on roads made treacherous by weather and the constant threat of attack. Reverend Taylor wrote in the fall of 1675, "summer coming opened a door unto that desolating war began by Philip, Sachem of the Pakoneket Indians . . . not so as that we should be wholly exempted from the fury of war, for our soil was moistened by the blood of three Springfield men, young Goodman Dumbleton, who came to our mill, and two sons of Goodman Brooks, who came here to look after the iron ore on the land he had lately bought of Mr. John Pynchon, Esq., who being persuaded by Springfield folk, went to accompany them, but fell in the way by the first assault of the enemy upon us, at which time they burnt Mr. Cornish's house to ashes and also John Sacket's with his barn and what was in it, being the first snowy day of winter; they also at this time lodged a bullet in George Granger's leg, which was the next morning taken out by Mr. Bulkley, and the wound soon healed. It was judged that the enemy did receive some loss at this time because in the ashes of Mr. Cornish's house were found pieces of the bones of a man lying about the length of a man in the ashes." Westfield was growing quickly, boasting a population of over five hundred people within the first twenty years.

Walter Lee was a colorful character in the early years of Westfield. On March 28, 1665, he was brought to court to answer charges "that he very seldom comes to God's ordinances on ye Lord's day, he not having been at ye meeting at Springfield from Feb. 8th to this tyme, and very seldom ye rest of ye winter past." James Cornish brought him to court "upon suspicion of killing a steer of his, ye said Mr. Cornish, at Woronoco, the summer past." An Irish servant of James Lyman was fined for calling Walter a "rogue, dog, rogue, and thief." Lee was fined twenty shillings "for his profaning the Lord's day at Woronoco this last winter, in that he thrashed corn on the Sabbath, which act he acknowledged to be so, and also for his calling Isaac Sheldon a member of old nick and a member of the Divell, and for his contempt of the authority in Springfield."

John Sacket brought a complaint against Walter Lee and Ambrose Fowler for "impounding his cattel." On September 27, 1670, Walter Lee brought suit against David Ashley "for taking ten shock of wheat last year and a load of Indian corn this year off [Lee's] land."

The Massachusetts General Court in Boston ordered the people of Westfield to move to Springfield in a letter dated March 20, 1676. With the dire threat of attack by the natives, it was felt that it would be easier to protect the greatest number of people if they were all gathered in one place. The people of Westfield strongly objected to this logic, sending a committee to the court to argue their case. The Reverend Edward Taylor penned the original plea, with Josiah Dewey, Isaac Phelps, and David Ashley signing the letter. They were successful in their case, but while the Westfield inhabitants could remain in their town, they were required to build a fortress large enough and strong enough to contain the entire population. More than two miles of walls were built to keep them safe, making sure the meetinghouse was contained within the walls. On March 21, 1700, "the inhabitants especially those that live on the Town plot . . . consider about fortifying for their security, did agree and vote that four houses should be securely fortified and Mr. Taylor's fort repaired if needed. The four houses agreed upon were those of John Weller, Stephen Kellogg, John Sacket, and Benjamin Smith, and also Consider Mosely." In November of 1723, the governor ordered Lieutenant Kellogg to raise a company to be partly stationed at Northfield and partly utilized for scouting, and sent him a captain's commission. The muster roll of this company which served from November 20, 1723, to May 30, 1724, contains the names of four Westfield men: David King, John Beamon, Jacob Wheeler, and David Sacket.

In order for a successful barter system to flourish, the value of currency must be agreed upon. In Westfield, prices were reset every year at the town meeting, based upon the crops gathered. For example, in 1688, a bushel of corn was valued at 2 shillings, peas at 3 shillings, wheat at 3 shillings 6 pence, and rye at 3 shillings. At the September 18, 1679, town meeting, James Cornish was to be paid eighteen pounds for keeping school the next year, paid in wheat, pork, and Indian corn in equal proportions.

Smoking in public has been a problem since the early days of the settlement. In 1644, Massachusetts passed a law stating "no person under the age of twenty-one years, nor any other that hath not accustomed himself to the use thereof, shall take any tobacko untill he hath brought a certificate under the hands of some who are approved for knowledge and skill in physick, that is needful for him, and allso that he hath received a lycense from the courte . . . no man within this colonye . . . shall take any tobacko publiquely in the street, highways, or any barn yards or open training days in any open places." On September 26, 1682, "Samuel Ely being complained of to this corte for that he contrary to the law did smoke tobacco in the street before his house, this corte doth sentence him to pay a fine of two shillings and six pence as a fine to the Countie Treasurer." Being a primarily agrarian society for many years, almost

everyone owned land dedicated to farming. Many of these farmers set aside an area to grow tobacco. By the mid 1800s tobacco was second only to whips in Westfield's economy. Leonard Atwater even combined the two, selling cigars and whips in a prosperous business venture.

On the other hand, liquor has been a mainstay of Westfield living since the very beginning. In 1668, Captain Aaron Cook was issued the first license to entertain travelers and sell liquor, and promptly opened up the first tavern in town. Just west of the old Mundale burying grounds stood the Farmers

Hotel for many years. In the mid 1800s, the Mountaineer Stage operated out of the hotel, running every day from Westfield to Sandisfield. Stephen Spelman ran the hotel from 1845 to 1853, selling out to William W. Bacon, who ran it until 1857, at which time it was sold to Miles Underhill.

In order for a plantation to be organized in the Massachusetts Bay Colony, land was to be reserved for clergy; finding and maintaining a clergyman was a priority of every community. Cornet Thomas Dewey invited the Reverend Edward Taylor to serve in Westfield. A cornet is a military title given to the color sergeant of the cavalry, and significant enough to be etched on Thomas' headstone. The corresponding position in the infantry was called an ensign.

John Munn received a land grant on February 7, 1670. Munn's Meadow (Woronoco Park) and Munn's Brook became landmarks in town, and the Mundale section hosted its own burying ground. By 1676, the population of Westfield had already reached one hundred fifty people. According to a Massachusetts law enacted in 1644, any community of at least fifty households was required to educate their children in reading and writing basics. In 1678, Westfield's first teacher, Mr. Denton, began teaching in local homes until the first eighteen square foot schoolhouse was built in 1701, near the meetinghouse.

In 1693, a member of Fearnot King's family was allowed to have "the use of what there is in our common . . . if he comes to town and sets up a bloomery and carries on the work." A bloomery is a pit or chimney in which wrought iron is produced, with heat resistant walls made of stone, clay, or earth. Air enters the bottom of the furnace through clay pipes, either by natural draft or forced by bellows. Iron ore and charcoal are introduced from the top into the hot furnace, and the small particles of iron fall to the bottom forming a spongy mass called the bloom. The holes of the bloom get filled with slag, and must be reheated and the slag hammered out; the final result is wrought iron. The next December, Fearnot was given permission to build a grist mill the following May on the stream above the meadow at Clay Hill. Fearnot King married Mary Fowler, daughter of Ambrose and Jane (Alvord) Fowler; together they had at least seven children. Brick kilns were built near Clay Hill, and the pines on the plains were used for rosum and turpentine.

The highway from Westfield to Springfield was laid out in 1673. Thomas Noble, Sr. was granted use of a half mile square in Four Mile Plains to make use of the pines for rosum for a period of three years. At the same meeting, a tract of land on Two Mile Brook was granted for the same purpose and length of time to Samuel Allen, Nathaniel Lee, and John Shepard. By doling out permission for use of small stands of pines, the town was hoping to preserve the trees for the future use of the townspeople. As early as 1696, a man was chosen every year to be "gager, viewer, searcher and surveyor of all turpentine, pitch, and rozem for the ensuing year." There was a penalty of five shillings established in April of 1704 for any new boxes made or old ones repaired for turpentine. Half of the fine went to the town, and the other half as a reward to the informer.

The famous Indian raid on Deerfield occurred in February of 1704. In May of that same year, there was an attack in what is now the Easthampton area by Indians headed for Westfield, but an abnormally wet spring made the flooding waters difficult to cross. The marauding band of Indians decided to concentrate on outlying settlements within easier reach away from the established walled fortresses, preying on unprotected settlers and travelers. As late as 1759, farmers chasing their cattle were still being scalped by the Indians in the outer commons, or the West Farms, as the Wyben area was called.

The Massachusetts General Court granted four hundred acres to "William Hubbard, Clerk of Westfield" in 1702 on "both sides of the Manhan River." When William Hubbard left to go to Enfield, he deeded the land to Isaac Sacket, which was then called Sacket's Farm until he died in 1709. When the common lands were divided among the settlers in 1734, a two and a half mile wide strip was formed in five sections, a half mile wide each, in the northern commons known as the Northampton Plains. The "Country Road to Northampton" formed the eastern border. Daniel Noble drew the first lot on the east side, followed by Lieutenant Thomas Ingersol, Edward Martindale, David Mosely, Mark Noble, Deacon Thomas Noble, Aaron Phelps, Samuel Bush, Isaac Fowler, and David Dewey.

Give Me That Old Time Religion

We think of the Puritans as coming to America to spread religious freedom. This could not be further from the historical truth. The Puritans wanted freedom to pursue their own religious practices, but refused to allow others that same right. Puritanism was actually repressive to the human spirit, while fostering narrowmindedness and fanaticism among its followers.

Westfield treasured its clergy. Despite being settled originally for commercial reasons, religion played a central role in its development. The first six ministers of the organized church served for a total of one hundred and ninety-five years. Once their roots were established here, none of them left to join another congregation and preach elsewhere. They are all buried in Westfield, and include the Reverends Edward Taylor, Nehemiah Bull, John Ballantine, Noah Atwater, Isaac Knapp, and Emerson Davis.

Reverend Edward Taylor, who served from 1679 to 1726, came from Harvard in the dead of winter, recording his observations along the way. Urged on by his respected friends, Cotton and Increase Mather of Boston, and Harvard president Charles Chauncey, Reverend Taylor reluctantly made the journey westward to accept the ministerial position. He describes crossing the crackling ice of the Connecticut River in December of 1671, staying at Captain Cook's place before moving in with Goodman Ashley, and biding his time until his residence could be erected. Captain Aaron Cook owned and operated Westfield's first "public house for the entertainment of strangers" from 1668 to 1676 before moving to Northampton. While in England, Taylor was "an ardent anti-monarchist, and his early writings are said to breathe in no doubtful terms his strong aversion to the rulings of the then existing dynasty." Educated for seven years at Cambridge University in England, and then for three more years at Harvard in Cambridge, Massachusetts, he became Westfield's lawyer, doctor, and farming consultant, performing these services as well as his ministerial duties. Five of his daughters married ministers, and his youngest son, Eldad, became a prominent member of Westfield society. Reverend Taylor's theology was strictly and devoutly orthodox Congregationalist, which ran headlong into conflict with the more liberal Reverend Solomon Stoddard from nearby Northampton.

Reverend Nehemiah Bull, who served from 1726 to 1740, was a missionary to the Housatonic Indians in the hills of western Massachusetts. As Reverend Taylor declined in his later years, Nehemiah became his assistant, before taking

over the congregation. He was also the grammar school master in 1724. When he died in 1740, his funeral sermon was preached by the Reverend Jonathan Edwards of Northampton, who was famous for the "Great Awakening."

Reverend John Ballantine, who served from 1740 to 1776, was a man of few words, so he made each one count. As he grew older, he began to write in his journal things he wouldn't say in town. In his journal on April 17, 1759, he wrote "John Ashley Esq died age 90. He has been Captain of a Company, Representative of the town many years; he outlived the expectations of his friends and even the desire of some of his relatives; he was as forgotten as one who has long been dead. Very few attended his funeral considering the number of his relatives and the offices he has held." On June 29, 1759, he wrote "I attended the funeral of Mrs. Abigail Fowler AEtat 55. She bore her distress very patiently, was willing to leave the world. She has been a very exemplary attender on the Public Worship. Very steadfast, not withstanding all the attempts of Seducers to draw her off. Very Savory in her Conversations, ready to help Neighbors in their difficulties. A great loss to survivors, but She, I trust, gains by Death." On July 31, 1766, he wrote "Attended the funeral of Deliverance Hanchett, aged 72, never married. Maintained by the town, unhappy in her temper, provoking in her language, lived undesired and died unlamented." On September 11, 1774, he wrote "attended the funeral of Jonathan Fowler who had almost completed his 89th year. He was a virulent opposer of ministers, differed from every one. He made a great deal of disturbance in his family for some years past by his provoking tongue. His wife and son have impatiently waited for his death. He lived undesired and dies unlamented." With such bluntness being recorded, it makes one wonder what was left unsaid.

Growing up in Boston, he was a graduate of Harvard in 1735, and served as pastor for thirty-five years in Westfield, living in the old Day house built by Deacon Thomas Noble. On June 6, 1769, he wrote, "President [Edward] Holyoke died, 1st Instant. President gave me 2 degrees, the 1st Commencement he officiated. He gave my son his first degree the last Commencement he officiated. He presided over the college 81 years." Religion played an important role in everyday life. On July 4, 1755, Reverend Ballantine met with Captain Ingersoll's company at the meetinghouse to pray for their safe return. Of course, times change, as he recorded on May 14, 1759, "Company met to enlist men. . . . Our men went away. There use to be a Sermon or prayers with them, but nothing of that Nature now, as if they had come to a conclusion it was in vain to Seek God." Homelessness has always been a concern, as he wrote on February 13, 1763, "A beggar lay by the fire, belonging to N. London. Its difficult to know ones duty to such persons. There are so many Impostors, knaves & cheats, kindness encourages them. Some of these get more and fare better than laborious men, which may tempt some to neglect labor and betake themselves to this mean practice. Every town should maintain their own poor . . . but to make a trade of Beggary should not be tolerated."

Reverend Noah Atwater, who served from 1781 to 1802, never preached the same sermon twice throughout his ministry, making it a practice to have each sermon prepared by Tuesday, allowing him the rest of the week for visiting his congregation and taking care of his domestic responsibilities. His published works include a book on nature. When he died he left a library of over one hundred and fifty-five books. His work with the local poor has been noted by contemporary writing. Reverend Atwater worked on the charter of the Westfield Academy, leaving them a legacy in his

estate. He recorded local events, as well. On August 23, 1786, he wrote "In the afternoon there was a remarkable thunder shower, with no very hard thunder, but a violent wind. It broke down the large tree before the meeting house door, also many Apple trees in the town, and leveled many fences, and broke considerable glass in the meeting house. It began to rain at exactly 5 o'clock, and rained 20 minutes, and the rain that fell was 1.7 inches. It was remarkably dark."

Reverend Isaac Knapp, who served from 1803 to 1847, was a peaceful, patient pastor, and was well-respected and well-liked throughout the community. His failing health in later years required an assistant, and for the first time the church Society helped to find a suitable helper.

Reverend Emerson Davis, who served from 1836 to 1866, was the first church leader in Westfield to be named by the church Society to his position. At one time he served as head of the Westfield Academy. When the normal school was established to train the teachers, Reverend Davis became the first principal of the school.

In 1754, there were one hundred fifty-seven families living in Westfield. This included eighteen widows, eight widowers, and thirty-eight "Separates." The average family size in this period was seven, so it would be safe to say that there were over one thousand people living here then. By the time of the first official census in 1790, Westfield boasted a population of two hundred and forty-eight families, in spite of the fact that Southwick and Montgomery, once part of Westfield, had become their own entities.

Separates, they called themselves Separate Baptists, were those who lived outside the mainstream Congregationalist church; they were not authorized by the standing ministry to preach in the community. Many of them were dismissed from the church in 1750 following strong disagreements over the taking of the Sacrament. The Separates believed that only those who had experienced the "new birth" were worthy of Communion, while the current belief of the time was that anyone of moral character and agreed to the Covenant could participate.

Teach the Children

Massachusetts has always focused on the education of its young as a way to improve the lives and minds of the populace. The law passed November 14, 1647, made towns of over fifty households liable to be fined for not appointing a person to teach their children to read and write. One of the main reasons for the law was to ensure that everyone could read the word of God. Part of the law reads, "It being one chief project of that auld deluder, Satan, to keep men from the knowledge of the Scriptures." Westfield has been a proud part of that tradition since its early years. In March, 1678, Lancelot Granger was called before the court "for neglecting to teach his children to write, but was discharged as he testified he was doing his best to teach them." The first teacher, Daniel Denton, was hired in 1678, and the first schoolhouse built in 1701 near the meetinghouse.

Lieutenant Samuel Root was deacon of the church from 1702 until his death in 1711, and owned an impressive library when he died. Some of the titles included in his estate, besides three bibles, were "Mourners Cordal, French Convert, Way to Blessing, How to Keep the Heart Blessed Remedy, Groans of the Damned, Baxters Now or Never, Catechisms, Military Discipline, Young Mans Guide, Discourse on Witchcraft, Barbarian Cruelty, Pilgrim's Guide, and Door of Salvation." Nehemiah Bull became the grammar school master in 1724. The Westfield Academy, based on the principles set forth by Benjamin Franklin in Philadelphia's academy, was the seventh academy chartered in Massachusetts, applying for a charter in 1793. It started on Broad Street on January 1, 1800, with fifteen prominent men from the local communities serving on its board of trustees. The original board consisted of the Reverend Noah

Atwater, the Honorable Samuel Fowler, the Honorable William Shepard, David Moseley, Abel Whitney, Samuel Mather, and Colonel James Taylor, all of Westfield; the Reverend Joseph Lathrop and Justin Ely of West Springfield; the Reverend Bezaleel Howard of Springfield; the Reverend Isaac Clinton of Southwick; the Reverend Solomon Williams and the Honorable Samuel Lyman of Northampton; the Reverend Joseph Badger of Blandford; and Jonathan Judd Jr. of Southampton. The trustees appointed a three member committee to assist the preceptor of the school, Peter Starr, of Middlebury, Vermont. Opening its doors to the first class of one hundred eighty-seven young men and women students eager to begin studying mathematics, language, bookkeeping, as well as practical and cultural subjects, the academy was poised to start turning out well-rounded educated members of society. The first school committee in town, consisting of the Reverend Isaac Knapp, Elder David Wright, Alfred Stearns, and Dr. William Atwater, was formed in 1824. The number of members on the committee varied, as the list in 1836 included William G. Bates, Jehiel Abbott and David Moseley.

The first normal school established with state funds in the United States opened in Barre, Massachusetts, in 1839. Its purpose was to train teachers for "common schools" in the commonwealth. The school ran for two years under the direction of Dr. Samuel P. Newman, until he died. A number of towns bid for the right to host the new school in their locale. Westfield's ultimately successful bid was led by the Reverend Emerson Davis, fourteen-year head of the Westfield Academy, and Attorney William Geltson Bates. Housed on the ground floor of the town hall, the school opened in Westfield in September of 1844, moving to its new building in 1846. The first full-time president of the school was David Rowe.

Books, used as a means of expanding the horizons of the people, have been available in Westfield for hundreds of years. Late in the 1700s, a group of prominent Westfield citizens, among them General William Shepard and Dr. Israel Ashley, Jr., formed a library for the elite of the community. In 1830, the Westfield Social Library was established by William G. Bates, and lasted about twenty years. Founding members paid five dollars per share, and nonmembers were allowed to borrow books if they could pay the rental fee. Among the original members were Norman T. Leonard, Esq., and Dr. Jehiel Abbott, an influential local physician.

In a casual conversation with Samuel Mather of Hartford, Henry B. Smith asked Mr. Mather why he so rarely visited Westfield. His reply was fortuitous for the town. To paraphrase Mr. Mather, unless one's destination is a tavern, Westfield has nothing to draw the casual traveler. "In fact, I will pledge ten thousand dollars for the maintenance of a public library if you can get one opened," he said. When Hiram Harrison heard this, he donated some land and a brownstone building on Main Street for the Athenaeum. The first organizational meeting was held on December 15, 1866, where it was decided that a lifetime directorship would cost five hundred dollars, and a lifetime membership would initially run fifty dollars. The original directors included William Bates, Henry Birch, and the Smith brothers, Samuel and Henry. Chosen to be the first librarian was the Reverend Sewall Lamberton. By 1899, delivery of books from the Athenaeum to the outlying areas had been established. The rural library in the Mundale section of town was run by W. E. Barnes, and the books were delivered by a horse drawn cart driven by C. W. Gibbs. In the Wyben area, the library was run by Grace G. Thompson and the books were delivered by S. A. Allen.

Travel Time

For many years, Westfield was an important crossroad. The road to Northampton ran through Westfield on its way from New Haven, Connecticut; many of Westfield's first settlers arrived via that highway. In the early 1800s, a large canal project followed that route, creating the Port of Westfield. From Boston, the post road ran through Westfield on the way to Albany, New York. When the first railroads were being built, it was only natural that they, too, would run through Westfield. By the time of the Civil War in 1860, the Western Railroad was running three trains a day east and west through town, while the Northampton and New Haven Railroad was running two trains a day north and south.

The Port of Westfield has a funny sound to it, with the town being so far from the ocean, but in 1822, the approval for the construction of a canal with access to New Haven made it a reality. Travel was finally made possible to the masses at a reasonable rate, and in a relatively comfortable manner. Road conditions were muddy in the spring and fall, dusty in the summer, and deep in snow in the winter, making spontaneous travel impossible. Trips were planned well in advance, and undertaken as a necessity. Canal passage from Westfield to New Haven began in 1829, and to

Northampton in 1835. Aurelias Taylor of Westfield was one of the passengers on a canal trip to New Haven in September of 1832, recording her experience in her diary. The ambitious canal project originally was intended to run all the way from New Haven to the St. Lawrence River on the Canadian border, but the advent of the railroad cut short its completion. Unforeseen obstacles uncovered by the existing length of canal would probably have ended the project before its target, even if the railroad had not come along. Water levels were difficult to maintain, dependable drivers hard to find, and unexpected winter shutdowns all added to the cost of running the canal. By the time the railroad opened on January 1, 1848, the canal was no longer needed.

At the town meeting of March 14, 1825, it was voted that "no person be allowed to pass upon any sidewalk with a horse or carriage, either by leading, driving or riding the same without incurring the penalty of one dollar." This was at a time when a day's wage for working on the highway was seventy-five cents from March to September, and fifty-eight cents from October to February. There were two hundred Irish immigrants in Westfield in 1826, hard at work laying the railroad down on its way to Northampton. The existing townspeople, being quiet, staid Anglo-Saxon Protestants for over one hundred and fifty years, found the loud, rambunctious Catholic Irish people difficult to comprehend. Commenting on the strange customs of foreigners, Reverend Ballantine wrote in his journal on July 1, 1761, "Some French neutrals here eat with us. Before they eat they murmur over a few words, &

cross themselves sitting. After eating they stood, their lips of them all moved, but nothing spoke audibly. They crossed themselves over Face and Breast." By 1850, more than one thousand people of Irish descent called Westfield home.

When your town is known as "Whip City" everyone would like to be able to take credit for its origin. The first whip business in Westfield is credited to Joseph Jakes in 1808. However, claims have been made that Titus Pease and Thomas Rose may have started their whip business as early as 1801. Hiram Hull began H. Hull and Son in 1810. As an inventor and innovator in the business, he soon introduced more scientific methods to produce superior whips and improve the manufacturing process at the same time. In 1821, he brought back a plaiting machine from a trip to Rhode Island, which inspired new ideas for Hiram. When the canal was completed to Westfield, Hull ran two boats a day to New Haven to ship merchandise for his general store located on the east side of the green. Earlier, D. L. Farnum had tried to make a plaiting machine with Henry Douglas and Samuel Lindsay after visiting a whip shop in Boston. By the early 1870s, the United States Whip Company in Westfield was producing more than twenty thousand whips per day.

There was one section of Westfield that earned the nickname "Ruinsville" by the sheer number of businesses that tried to survive in that location, only to fail. One of the most famous businessmen to attempt success there was Cyrus Field, who later became known for laying the transatlantic cable to England. Located about one-half mile west of the Stevens Paper Company, the first failure was a carding mill, built in the 1830s by John Shepard. On May 13, 1840, the mill was sold to Cyrus Field. Westfield Paper Mill soon bought it, but sold it in 1856 to Warren Whitman, who manufactured cotton goods there, including twine, mops, and clothesline. Following Whitman's failure, the mill was sold to Josiah Knowles who turned it into a whip factory. In 1881, Frank and Lazene Osden purchased the business and it became Osden Brothers Whips. The end of the line came in 1891, when the building burned down.

Entertainment occasionally arrived in Westfield, as Reverend Ballantine wrote on August 10, 1773, "Dr. Anthony Yeldal set up a stage. On it 2 lads entertained the Spectators by walking on their hands & by various feats of activity. Then the Doctor harangues on what he can do, the terms on which he doth any thing. The way he goes on in. He harangues on the Virtues of certain medicines he hath to Sell. There was not a large collection of people. He is to appear on 5 Tuesdays."

There were men of foresight in Westfield, as evidenced by town meeting notes of May 9, 1745, when it was voted that "Lieutenant David Mosely, John Bancroft, and Stephen Nash be a committee to take care speedily that the mill dams standing on the Westfield River both in Westfield and Springfield have so much of them pulled down as shall be sufficient for the fish to pass up sd. river."

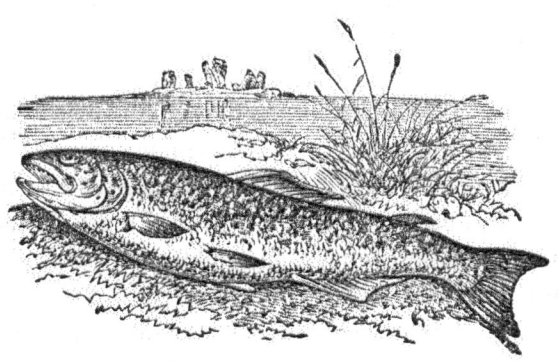

The Sounds of War

Notes from the town meetings in 1743 show a widespread dissatisfaction with a new law ordering towns to "mark and preserve as masts for the Royal Navy, all pine trees twenty-four inches in diameter, twelve feet above the ground." The law was so unpopular that it was basically ignored.

Westfield has contributed more that its share to the war efforts through the years. On September 7, 1755, a battle at Fort William Henry raged on for more than four hours; forty-six men, including Major Noah Ashley, Captain Jonathan Ingersoll, and Private Richard Campbell, all of Westfield, died. Following the surrender of Fort William Henry in 1757, the survivors were given safe conduct back to their homes by the French. Instead, the Indians, and some French soldiers, ignored that order and massacred troops, women, and children. Two men from Westfield were among those slaughtered, William Kerr and Shem Kellogg. On July 3, 1770, Reverend Ballantine visited the Widow Kerr, "Last Friday her son Joseph unyoking cattle having freed one from the yoke the chain fasted about his leg. The ox drew him about 17 rods on his back, which occasioned his death last Saturday. I baptised him, 1755." The widow Katherine Kerr died on November 29, 1817, at the age of 98 years. Her daughter, Anne Kerr, never married and died September 28, 1836, aged 96 years.

One of the ironies of the American Revolution is that for the first one hundred years of its existence, America had more freedom and input into local government than free Englishmen of the time. When that was no longer enough, the men of Westfield joined their comrades in the crusade for independence. On June 7, 1774, Captain John Mosely and Elisha Parks were elected to the Massachusetts Assembly. Joining them in September of that year, at the County Congress in Northampton, was Eldad Taylor, the fourteenth child of Westfield's first pastor, Edward Taylor. Eldad was town clerk in Westfield for over thirty years, and died in Boston of smallpox in 1777. Ensign Zachariah Bush, Dr. Israel Ashley, Aaron Bush, Lieutenant Daniel Sacket, and Aaron King were all chosen to serve on the Committee of Correspondence on July 5, 1775.

From the British viewpoint, one of the most frustrating aspects of the American Revolution was finding the American army. Many of the battles were fought by the militia, who were called to duty as needed, much like our current National Guard, and returned to their farms after the battle. Most of the enlistments were of short duration, making it difficult for the British to determine which farmers were fighting, and which ones were simply minding their farms. Ensign Zachariah Bush, Sergeants Benjamin and Moses Dewey, Captain Roger Noble, drummer Ruggles Winchell, Gideon Shepard, and Asa Noble were all discharged after serving three weeks and one day following the march to Lexington. On April 20, 1775, the "Muster Roll of the Minute Company that came from Westfield" consisted of Lieutenant John Shepard, 2nd Lieutenant Zachariah Bush, Sergeant J. Benjamin Dewey, Sergeant Gideon Shepard, Sergeant Asa Noble, Corporal Israel Sackett, Corporal Roger Noble, Corporal Benjamin Winchell, Corporal James Nimocks, drummer Ruggles Winchell, fifer Jedediah Taylor, William Welch, James Colverson, James Derrick, Jared Plumb, Stephen Dewey, David Taylor, William Robinson, Martin Root, Eliah Dewey, Ashbel Noble, Abijah Dewey, Aaron Chapman, David Ross, J. Snell, John Smith, Ignatius Lines, Joshua Senn, Solomon Williams, Lewis Charles, Luther White, Martin Dewey, Moses Gunn, Phineas Sexton, John Dewey, David Piercy, Abner Ward, Moses Bush, Asahel Owen, David King, Abner Sackett, Justice Pomeroy, Nathaniel Truman, Warham Gunn, Daniel Gunn, Reuben

Wharfield, Joss Kellogg, Eli Granger, Bartholomew Noble, Amos Bush, and Asah Mosely. Nineteen soldiers were credited with traveling two hundred and twenty-four miles at a penny a mile for a total of eighteen shillings and eight pence.

In the beginning of the American Revolution, Hampden Park in Springfield was the collection point and the training grounds for the local militia of western Massachusetts, including Company K of Westfield. It was customary at that time for the men of the regiment to elect their captains and their lieutenants. Despite the fact that the men chose Pliny Wood to lead them by more than a two-thirds vote, Andrew Campbell was appointed lieutenant, causing such an uproar that the men left the training ground and returned home to Westfield. Captain Briggs sent troops to arrest Company K and force them to return to Springfield. Before a confrontation could occur, a compromise was reached and David Chase was appointed First Lieutenant, joining Captain Lucius Walkley and Lieutenant Edwin T. Johnson to lead the volunteers of Westfield in the fight for independence.

Richard Falley, brother-in-law to Zachariah Bush and great-grandfather to President Grover Cleveland, became the fourteenth armorer to the continental army. Paid forty shillings per month, his duties included maintaining and repairing the army's muskets. Prior to the start of the conflict, Falley built an armory on Moose Meadow Brook in Westfield, producing top quality muskets for the local militia. As a boy, he was captured by the Indians and held for ransom. His father, Richard Falley Sr., was kidnapped as a boy and sold into slavery in Boston.

Sworn by Eager Noble to Justice of the Peace Patrick Boise on September 17, 1838:

I, Eager Noble of Westfield in the county of Hamden of Massachusetts depose and say that I was seventy-eight years old the sixteenth day of May last - that I was acquainted with Jacob Noble from the time he was a boy till his death - and I further testify that said Jacob Noble enlisted in the service in the War of Revolution the sixteenth day of May in the year 1776, if I remember correctly, I enlisted the same time. We inlisted under Captain John Gray - Lieutenant Silas Foseln - and our colonel's name was Woodbridge - said Jacob and myself marched to Tyconderoga - about the first of August 1776. I should think we remained in the service there till about the first day of December there following - while we were at Tyconderoga Arnold was defeated by the British on the lakes - no serious engagement was had with the enemy during this campaign. I further state that said Jacob again inlisted in the service in the summer of 1777 - it was about harvest time. I inlisted at the same time. Our officers Colonel John Mosely - Captain David Mosely - Lieutenant Zachariah Bush - we marched from Westfield through Pittsfield, New Lebanon, the furthest place to which we marched was to Fort Edward - I think said Jacob was out in the service at this time six or seven weeks - said Jacob again inlisted the time I cannot recollect I think it was in the fall of the same year. I inlisted but did not go with him. Colonel Brown was the colonel killed at Stone Robby. Said Jacob has often told me he was in the battle at Stone Robby others have told me the same. Said Jacob showed me on his return some blood on his clothes of Jared Noble his cousin who was killed in this battle. I feel confident that this last enlistment and service were for the period of three months. I further state that said Jacob was with me to guard some prisoners in Westfield about three weeks.

The war years were not easy ones for the families remaining here in Westfield. In a letter dated April 14, 1782, David Mosely wrote "We are raising up men to fill the Continental army though we go on slowly, we have 6 men to raise but have but 2 engaged yet. Have something further to inform you of though I do it with reluctance. I had the sheriff near me and he has taken away one of my family to jail for debt, about three weeks ago; which is David King. As times are hard and money scarce I look upon it as a loud call to me to be also ready. I remember your caution which was to live short, which I think was needless for poverty has got such a hold on me that I am obliged to do it. "

The United States suffered growing pains following the successful conclusion of the War of Independence. After fighting for their new country, many western Massachusetts farmers returned to their homes to find their land and possessions saddled with debt. Merchants had extended credit to the soldiers' families and expected repayment upon their return. Raging inflation had destroyed the value of the paper money issued by the government in payment for military service. In order to satisfy their debts, many former soldiers were forced to sell their land at less than a third of its face value. As a result, they lost their right to vote, since property ownership was a requirement for that privilege. Penniless yeomen had their lands confiscated or were sentenced to jail. In the summer of 1786, local veterans Daniel Shays of Pelham, Eli Parsons of Chicopee, and Luke Day of West Springfield, angered and frustrated by the fact that they had just finished fighting the British to prevent this sort of mistreatment, called their comrades back to arms in protest. It is estimated that over nine thousand former soldiers, who called themselves "Regulators," responded to the call. Gathering in large groups, they prevented the justices from sitting in the debtors courts; keeping some of their friends out of jail, and freeing others already there. Despite rumors to the contrary, the confrontations initially caused very few casualties and very little damage. The Regulators did cause concerns for local officials, state government, and as far away as the newly formed national confederate government. People like George Washington, Thomas Jefferson, and Samuel Adams were keeping a close watch on the proceedings in western Massachusetts in these troubled times, fearing an eruption into a major civil war. George Washington wrote, "What a triumph for the advocates of despotism, to find that we are incapable of governing ourselves and that systems founded on the basis of equal liberty are merely ideal and fallacious." Thomas Jefferson wrote, "A little rebellion now and then is a good thing. It is a medicine necessary for the sound health of government." Samuel Adams wrote, "Rebellion against a king may be pardoned, or lightly punished, but the man who dares to rebel against the laws of a republic ought to suffer death." Controversial and unpopular Governor James Bowdoin of Massachusetts felt that "the benefits of the Revolution are being undone by knaves and thieves who intend tyranny."

Since the Massachusetts General Court was sympathetic to the Regulators and funds were tight, it would not agree to raise a state militia to combat the Regulators. After months of frustrating failure, Governor Bowdoin and some eastern bankers decided to raise a private army in December of 1786, hiring over four thousand mercenaries led by General Benjamin Lincoln, to put down the growing mass of Regulators. When the Regulators learned of this new army, they decided to arm themselves by raiding the federal armory in Springfield. On January 25, 1787, the Regulators trudged through four feet of snow towards the target. General William Shepard of Westfield, occupying the armory to safeguard it from the rebels, led the militia. By firing into the crowd of protesters, Shepard succeeded in quelling the rebellion.

When founding patriot John Hancock beat Governor Bowdoin in the next election, he inherited the dilemma of what to do with the rebels who had been condemned to hang. The day of the scheduled execution, June 21, 1787, the prisoners were marched out to the gallows. At the very last instant, the governor reprieved the condemned men. Shays' Rebellion had a profound influence on the Federal Convention in the summer of 1787. One of the direct results of the uprising was the abolition of the Articles of Confederation and the creation of the United States Constitution, thus forming a strong federal government with the ability to respond quickly to armed insurrections aimed against it.

The Rhode Island legislature spent two years voting against the Constitution a total of thirteen times, before finally ratifying it in 1790, one year into George Washington's presidency, by a total of two votes. New Hampshire had approved it on June 21, 1788, making it the law of the land.

The Gravestone Carvers

Local quarries were home to numerous stone carvers whose works adorn our nearby burying grounds. Find the quarry, find the carver, was the refrain often heard when researching the location of early colonial gravestone carvers. When you stop to think about it, this is just common sense. Transportation was limited and cumbersome, while the sheer size and weight of gravestones meant the likelihood of finding the carver near the source of material was great. Many of the early carvers actually owned all or part of the quarries where they found their best stone for their customers.

The Connecticut River valley is abundant with sandstone. A sedimentary rock lain down during the time of the dinosaurs, it is commonly referred to as red sandstone and brownstone. Schist is a metamorphic rock that comes in almost infinite variety. The word schist comes from the ancient Greek for "split" which describes its formation from a multitude of minerals, as well as its tendency to split after many years of exposure to the New England elements; its appearance displays a sparkly effect when the light is just right. Slate was quarried locally, but was mainly imported from the Boston quarries. Marble began to be imported and become popular in the early 1800s. It is said that the white of the marble represented the purity of the soul, and being easier to carve made it a favorite with the local carvers. However, the Industrial Revolution was coming soon, and the resultant acid rain interacted with the marble headstones, "sugaring" the surface and making many epitaphs illegible.

George Griswold was one of the earliest identified gravestone carvers in the Connecticut River valley. He carved in stone from the Windsor, Connecticut, quarries in the late 1600s. An example of his carving can be seen on Edward Griswold's stone on page 101.

Joseph Nash carved out of Hadley, Massachusetts. His career spanned the early 1700s and, despite his simple and conservative style of lettering, proved to be quite popular. Many of his headstones appear in Westfield, including the one for David Ashley on page 55.

The Thomas Johnson family produced gravestones around Middletown, Connecticut, for a hundred years. They owned and worked stone pits known locally as the Johnson quarries. They influenced the work of many subsequent carvers in the Connecticut River valley. The elder Thomas exhibited a skilled arrangement of elements on his stones, and the quality of his lettering shows care and attention to detail rarely found earlier. Joseph Johnson worked for a number of years out of the Windsor, Connecticut quarries. You can see an example of his work on the Ashley children's stone on page 52.

William Holland was an apprentice under Joseph Johnson and had a fairly short carving career, but was very influential in the area. Beginning his career in Middletown, he soon moved to the Longmeadow area in Massachusetts in the mid 1700s. While there, it appears he trained numerous carvers in the trade. You can see his work on the Jonathan Weller stone on page 135.

Joseph Williston was one of the carvers heavily influenced by Holland. His shop was located in Springfield,

Massachusetts, approximately at the end of the current Liberty Street. One of the distinctive features of his work has been called the "monkey paw nose" on his cherubs. His was a very short career, ending with his death in 1768, which produced a large quantity of stones, one of which is the Hannah Mosely stone on page 89.

John Ely of West Springfield began carving in the late 1760s. His shop was located almost directly across the Great River from Williston's shop. With a distinctive high relief cherub, Ely's work can be found in numerous burying grounds in the valley. Working with Longmeadow sandstone, much of his work is still pristine after 250 years. An example of his carving can be seen on the Warham Parks stone on page 132.

Ezra Stebbins began a prolific carving shop in Longmeadow in the mid-1700s and his early work appears to be influenced by William Holland. There are numerous gravestones from the Stebbins shop in Westfield, including the Reverend John Ballantine stone on page 119.

Hermon Newell is one of local researchers' favorite carvers, simply because he signed so many of his stones, making identification easy. Based in Longmeadow, he appears to have been trained in the Stebbins shop. You can find a sample of his carving on the Josiah Scovel stone on page 143.

Solomon Brewer was an extremely talented carver who grew up in Springfield. He began carving in the late 1760s and worked in Massachusetts for a short time before the war. After serving in the Revolutionary War, he moved his family to southern Connecticut, and then to New York. An example of one of his first carvings can be seen on the Ezra Clap stone on page 131.

Nathaniel Phelps had a prolific carving career based out of Northampton, working between 1750 and the early 1770s, when he went bankrupt. He was a dominant carver in the Northampton area until the Revolutionary War. An example of his carving can be seen on the Samuel Fowler stone on page 99.

Thomas Spelman was raised in Middletown, Connecticut. The proliferation of gravestone carvers in the area during his formative years very likely influenced his choice of careers. Shortly after his marriage in 1732, he moved to Durham, where his wife's family lived. While there, he established a reputation as a competent gravestone carver. In the early 1750s he moved to Granville, Massachusetts, where he continued to carve, gaining the respect of the neighboring towns. An example of his carving can be seen on the Mary Bush stone on page 129.

Aaron Bliss commonly carved his gravestones from a chocolate colored stone quarried out of the Wilbraham area. His cherubs have wings which resemble a beagle's floppy ears. In Westfield, his work also appears on red sandstone, likely originating from the Longmeadow quarries. An example of his carving can be seen on the Edward Martindale stone on page 125.

The Gravestone Symbols

In the beginning, there was the Holy Bible. It affected every aspect of daily life and death in colonial America. The early settlers took the commandment to "erect no graven images" literally, and many of the oldest graves were marked only by a plain fieldstone. Wooden markers were later used to identify burial sites. However, wood was ephemeral, "headboards" lasted no longer than five years in New England, and so stone became the carving material of choice. The first gravestones contained only the written word, with no adornment and no images.

Gravestones were very expensive, so only the richer and more educated members of the community had them erected. Macabre engravings of grinning skulls were among the first images to appear on the stones. Death's heads were mortality symbols, not religious, and so were acceptable to the strict Puritan ethic.

Soul effigies, or cherubs, gradually began to evolve from the bare-boned skulls of the death's heads. The mid-1700s saw an evolution of religious beliefs in the Great Awakening, and the local gravestones reflected that growth. The faces began to appear more lifelike, with eyes, hair, and facial expressions. Some tympanums even sported primitive portraits.

Right around the turn of the 19th century, religious imagery began to disappear. The Greek and Roman republics of ancient history influenced the young country; carvings of the old-world willow and urn motif dominated the graveyards in the early 1800s. Meanwhile, marble was replacing sandstone as the preferred stone. It was a softer stone, making it easier to carve. There was obvious beauty in the purity of the bright, white marble, but when the Industrial Revolution arrived in the mid 1800s, the gravestones began to dissolve at a rapid pace. The acid rain chemically reacted with the marble stone, and soon made much of the lettering and imagery indecipherable.

Obelisks of sandstone and marble appeared in local cemeteries in the mid 1800s. Popular in Europe after Napoleon brought one back to France as a present for Josephine, America adopted the style quickly. One monument, taking up a small amount of ground space, could contain a large amount of family information.

The Ashleys

Smallpox was a virulent disease that struck colonial communities with deadly force. An outbreak in the springtime of 1722 caused numerous deaths in Westfield, and the town voted to "send to Roxbury for Dr. Thomson . . . to Wethersfield for some nurse, and to keep a day of humiliation for God's hand against us in the small pox." Aaron Noble, 25 years old, died of smallpox just five days after returning from the Quebec campaign in 1760. It even became the topic of discussion at the town meeting in April of 1777. The houses of the Sacket brothers served as smallpox inoculation centers in 1778 under the supervision of an oversight committee consisting of Dr. Samuel Mather, Captain David Mosely, Lieutenant Richard Falley, and Elisha Parks, Esq. Doctors of the time were helpless against the disease, including Dr. Israel Ashley, considered one of the top physicians in the area. He lost seven children under the age of six, and died of smallpox in Stillwater, New York, while serving as chief surgeon under Colonel William Williams on August 2, 1758. From January 5th through the 8th of 1743, Reverend Ballantine mentions in his journal that he prayed at Dr. Ashley's house and at the funeral of his children. One of them died while he was praying with them. The stone with Dr. Ashley's three children was carved by an itinerant carver, Joseph Johnson.

Dr. Israel Ashley was the grandson of one of Westfield's first settlers, David Ashley, and graduated from Yale in 1731. He married Margaret Mosely on November 20, 1735. Together they had at least nine children including Elizabeth on September 26, 1736; Israel on November 22, 1737; Ezra on February 3, 1739; Solomon on September 20, 1741; Theodosia on November 1, 1743; Margaret on September 3, 1746; Israel Jr. on June 15, 1747; Solomon on January 20, 1749; Theodosia on January 2, 1751; and twins Thomas and William on May 18, 1752. Dr. Ashley was town treasurer from 1733 to 1758, deacon of the church from 1746 to 1755, and elected selectman on five different occasions.

Daughter Margaret married Jonathan Dwight on October 29, 1766, in Boston. Together they had at least eight children including Lucinda born on September 10, 1767; James on July 5, 1769; Margaret on February 5, 1771; Jonathan on December 28, 1772; Edmund on January 19, 1774; Sophia on September 4, 1776; Edmund on November 28, 1780; and Henry on June 25, 1783.

Israel Jr. became a doctor like his father, graduating from Yale in 1767, and then studying medicine in Springfield, served as selectman numerous times, and married Mary Gelston on February 10, 1774. They had at least six children including Israel born on August 13, 1776; Mary on August 21, 1778; Margaret on November 11, 1780; Harriet on February 27, 1783; Hannah on April 23, 1785; and Thomas on March 16, 1788. Young Israel died in 1800 while hunting deer when his gun discharged by accident. Doctor Israel died of fever on March 25, 1814, and his wife died just one week later on April first, which may explain why no stones are found in their memory.

The Ashley family was one of the seven most influential in the Connecticut River valley in the late 1600s and early 1700s. Besides the Ashleys, the families referred to as the "River Gods" were the Pynchons, Stoddards, Dwights, Porters, Partridges, and Williams, each including numerous members of the clergy, military, and political factions in the region. Westfield settler David Ashley was a twin, born to Robert and Mary Ashley at nine o'clock in the morning in 1642. His twin sister died shortly after birth. David married Hannah Glover of New Haven on November 24, 1663, in Springfield, where they lived for a little over three years. David's father was awarded a land grant in Woronoco which David acquired and eventually settled in 1667, near the juncture of the Great and Little Rivers. In 1669, David Ashley and Joseph Whiting were granted the right to build a gristmill on Sackett's Creek. Walter Lee brought a court action against David on September 27, 1670, accusing him of taking wheat and corn from his land. The case was settled before the jury came to a verdict. When Reverend Taylor came to Westfield in December of 1671, he spent his first evening with the Ashleys. The Reverend wrote in his diary "We went to Mr. Whiting's. There the men of the town came to welcome me, and after supper I went to Goodman Ashley's, where I was till Mr. Whiting had got his house ready that I might be with him." During the town meeting held November 18, 1696, "it is voted Left [Lt.] Samuel Root, Nathaniel Bancroft, Adijah Dewey, and David Ashley should be as a comitey to prise all lands in Westfield, and stock all yt is above one year old, and yt all heads should bee apprised at ten pound pr head to defray town charges."

Towards the end of the Queen Anne's War, the Ashley house was one of those ordered to be fortified for safety by the town on June 9, 1712. David served the town of Westfield as a juror, selectman, and treasurer. He took the oath of the freeman at a court session in Springfield on September 28, 1680. Together David and Hannah had at least eleven children including Samuel on October 16, 1664; David on March 10, 1666; John on June 27, 1669; Joseph on July 31, 1671; Sarah on September 19, 1673; twins Hannah and Mary on December 14, 1675; Jonathan on June 21, 1678; Abigail on April 27, 1681; Mary on March 3, 1683; and Rebecca on May 30, 1685.

Barrelmaker David Jr.'s will contains details of some of the land he owned in Westfield, when he granted:

In the name of God Amen. The twentieth day of June in the year of our Lord 1739, I David Ashley of

Westfield, in the county of Hampshire, in the Province of Massachusetts Bay, in New England. Cooper, being in considerable good measure of Health & of perfect Mind and Memory, thanks be given unto God therefore, calling unto mind the mortality of my Body & knowing that it is appointed for all men once to die do make & ordain this my Last will & Testament . . .

Imprimis: I give & bequeath to Mary just my Dearly beloved wife the sum of fifty Pounds Current money and the improvement of one-half of my dwelling house and Barn with half the Lot where the house and Barn Standeth & one third part of my other land that is not disposed of & the improvement of one-third part of all my personal Estate, so long as she remains my widow and I likewise give her my Bay Mare that is a pacer to her dispose.

Item: I give to my wellbeloved son Thomas Ashley one-half of my land on the West side of Simsbury road in the outer Commons & Ten acres of Land on the East side of Simsbury road joining to his own land & twenty acres of land more on the east side of Simsbury road out of my lot there, that was part of my right in that Division & he shall take it on the Southerly Side of Sd. Lot next to John Root's land, in the outer Commons, & I likewise give him two lots on Mungo Hill, in the inner Commons, one of Sd. lots was laid out to Lieut. Jonathan Ashley the other side of sd. lots was laid out to Daniel Gunn, be them more or less.

Item: I give to my wellbeloved son David Ashley one-half of my land on the West side of Simsbury road in the outer Commons & half of my lot on Mungo Hill in the inner Commons & I likewise give him my lot on the East side of Simsbury road in the outer Commons excepting twenty acres I have given to son Thomas Ashley.

Item: I give to my wellbeloved son Moses Ashley one-half of my lot between the rivers near the West Mountain in the inner Commons. . . .

Item: I give to my four sons, that is to Thos., David, Moses and Israel Ashley all the rest of my out Lands that I have not in particular give & disposed of & leave it with them to divide it to & among themselves as they shall think Just & reasonable. The Gristmill I give to my three eldest sons, that is Thomas, David, and Moses Ashley.

Item: my further will & pleasure is that the aforesd. Legacies be pd. out of my personal estate that is now already disposed of & the rest if any there be to be divided to & among my four sons equally, the Legacies to be paid either in the personal estate or in Bills of Credit old tenore. I likewise constitute & appoint my four sons that is Thomas Ashley, David Ashley, Moses Ashley, and Israel Ashley to being Executors of this my last will & Testament, & I do hereby utterly disavow, revokde, & disanul all & every other former Testaments, wills, & legacies, bequests & Executions by me in any way before named and bequeathed, satisfying & confirming this & no other to be my last will & Testament in witness whereof I have hereunto So Set my hand & seal this day & year above written.

Abigail Dewey died of pleurisy just four years later. Thomas died on August 25, 1755, when he fell off a cart of hay.

Captain John Ashley headed west, supervising the settlement of the Housatonic valley, including Sheffield and Great Barrington. He married Sarah Dewey on September 8, 1692. Together they had at least eight children including Sarah born on September 27, 1693; Hannah on December 18, 1695; John on October 19, 1697; Moses on October 1, 1700; Ebenezer on March 29, 1702; June 15, 1704; Roger on January 30, 1705; and Lydia on April 11, 1708.

Elizabeth Ashley, daughter of David and Mary (Dewey) Ashley, was born on March 3, 1697 and married James Dewey on May 15, 1718. Together they had at least nine children including Stephen born on March 13, 1719; Elizabeth on September 29, 1722; Anna on August 30, 1724; Keziah on October 20, 1726; Daniel on March 10, 1729; James on August 14, 1731; Josiah on January 29, 1733; Mary on April 6, 1735; and Josiah on September 8, 1737. Her great, great-grandson was John 'the Educator' Dewey, who was also known as the 'American Father of Education.' He was an author, philosopher, psychologist, humanist, and educator; serving as a teacher at the University of Michigan, the University of Chicago, and Columbia University. John wrote "The self is not something ready-made, but something in continuous formation through choice of action." He believed that "since there is no single set of abilities running throughout human nature, there is no single curriculum which all should undergo. Rather, the schools should teach everything that anyone is interested in learning." His works include "Logical Conditions of a Scientific Treatment of Morality" in 1903, and "Democracy and Education" in 1916.

Abigail was the daughter of Jonathan Ashley and Abigail Stebbins, whose father was Benjamin Stebbins of Springfield. Abigail was the firstborn child of the Ashleys, and never married. Her brother Jonathan attended Yale, graduating with three of his cousins, Israel, John, and Joseph Ashley in 1730, in a class of eighteen. He was the second ordained minister in Deerfield, Massachusetts, marrying Dorothy Williams, daughter of the Reverend William Williams of

Hatfield. Being a devout Tory, Jonathan preached from his pulpit about the sins of plotting against the king. The week after the fighting at Concord and Lexington, Jonathan's sermon promised the congregation that the Sons of Liberty would eternally burn in hell for their rebellious behavior. Unfortunately for him, the town consisted of faithful patriots and the following week Jonathan found the pulpit boarded shut, and his salary suspended. It was a difficult time for everyone, and his wife Dorothy attempted suicide twice during that period.

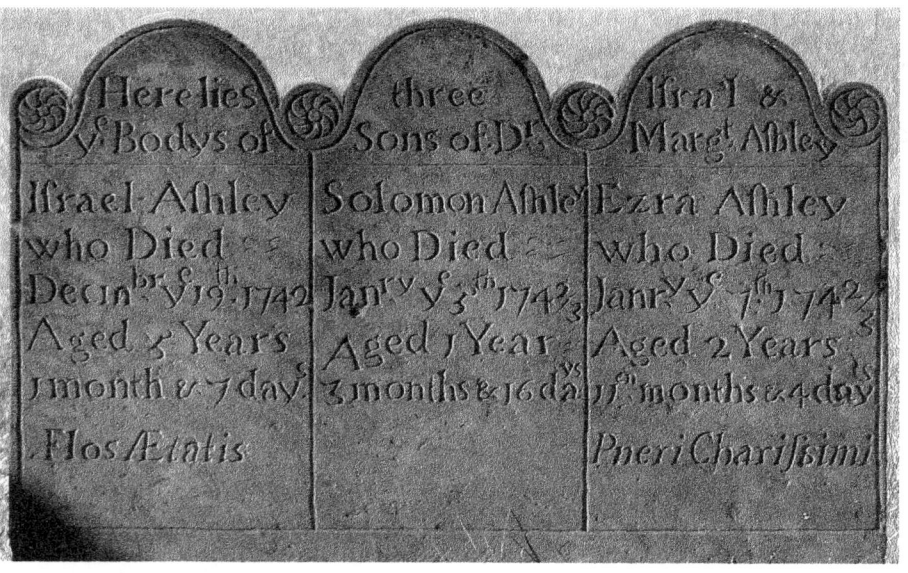

Here lies ye bodys of
three sons of Dr
Isra'l & Margt Ashley

Carved by Joseph Johnson

Israel Ashley
who Died
Decmbr ye 19th 1742
Aged 5 Years
1 month & 7 days
Flos AEtatis

Solomon Ashley
who Died
Janry ye 5th 1742/3
Aged 1 Year
3 months & 16 days

Ezra Ashley
who Died
Janry ye 7th 1742/3
Aged 2 Years
11 months & 4 days
Pueri Charissimi

In memory of Israel
Ashley Esqr who being
abroad in the Public
Service as Surgeon
of a rigement Died at
Still waters Augt 2d 1758
in ye 47th Year of his Age

Procrastination is the Thief of
time Year after Year it steals,
til all is fled. And to the
mercies of a moment leaves
the vast concerns of an
Eternal scene.
Also in memory of his
four Infant Children
named Theodosia
Solomon, Thomas
& Sophia.

Carved by Aaron Bliss

In memory of
Mr Israel Ashley
Junr son of
Doctr Israel and
Mrs Mary Ashley
who died
29th May 1800
in the 24th Year
of his age.

To mortals & their
hopes I bid adue
and ask no more
the rising sun to
view

Carved by John Ely

MR
DAVID
ASHLEY
DYED ON DEC'R
YE 18, 1718 AGED
77 YEAR

Carved by Joseph Nash

In memory of
John
Ashley Esqr
who died
April ye 16th
1759 in ye
90th year of
his age

Carved by Joseph Williston

In memory of
Mrs Margaret
Ashley who
died 25th July
1791 in the 77th
Year of her Age

Life is a bubble
quickly broke
A tale forgot
as soon as spoke
A shadow changing
with the sun
which spreads itself
and then is gone.

Carved by John Ely

Mr ROGER
ASHLEY Son
to John Ashley
Esq Died Feb
ye 10th 1738
Aged 33

Carved by Nathaniel Phelps

The Deweys

Cornet Thomas, born to Thomas and Frances (Clark) Dewey on February 16, 1639, in Windsor, Connecticut, married Constant Hawes on June 1, 1663. Together they had at least 10 children, including Thomas born on March 26, 1664; Adijah on March 5, 1666; Mary on January 28, 1668; Samuel on June 25, 1670; Hannah on February 21, 1672; Elizabeth on January 10, 1677; James on July 3, 1678; Abigail on February 14, 1680; James on November 12, 1683; and Israel on July 9, 1686. Thomas paid six shillings on January 18, 1660, for the privilege of sitting in the 'long seats' in the meetinghouse in Windsor. On November 12, 1662, he was granted a homelot of four acres in Northampton, Massachusetts. Four years later, on July 6, 1666, he was granted thirty acres in Westfield, then a part of Springfield. It seems he had finally found the home he had been seeking, becoming a prominent citizen of the new town, serving on the committee sent to Springfield in 1669, petitioning to become a separate town. Thomas is listed as a farmer and miller in the Little River district in Westfield.

Captain Adijah, born to Thomas and Constance (Hawes) Dewey on March 5, 1666, married Sarah Root in 1688. In 1702, Adijah was named tithingman and in 1718 he became a deacon of the church. Together Adijah and Sarah had at least nine children, including Thomas born on January 9, 1691; Adijah Jr. on September 30, 1693; Sarah on March 17, 1695; Esther on January 20, 1698; Mary on September 18, 1701; Abigail on January 28, 1703; Bethiah on August 11, 1706; and twins Moses and Ann on January 6, 1714.

From the Captain's will:

> . . . the twenty third day of March one Thousand Seven Hundred & thirty three I Adijah Dewey of Westfield . . . being sensible of my own Mortality knowing that it's appointed for all men once to dye & now at this time of Perfect Mind & Memory & in some good measure of Health, thanks be given to God for the same I do therefore make & ordain this my last Will & Testament (Viz.) Principally & first of All I recommend my Soul into the hands of God that Gave it & my body I recommend to the Earth to be buried in a Decent Christian Manner at the Discretion of my Christian friends & relations nothing doubting but at the resurrection I shall receive the same again by the Mighty Power of God & as touching Such Worldly Estate wherewith it has pleased God to bless me with in this life I give demise and Dispose of the Same in the following Manner.

Born in Windsor, Connecticut, in 1675, David Dewey was chosen constable for the town in 1705, served as selectman in 1708, and was chosen deacon in 1712. Primarily a weaver, he and his wife Sarah had at least five children, including David born on June 28, 1700; Charles on July 18, 1703; Nathaniel on September 21, 1706; Isaac on September 10, 1708; and Sarah on May 16, 1711. We discover some colonial beliefs in the wording of David's last will and testament:

> being weak in body but of sound and good understanding . . . fully believing yt it shall by his grace have a blessed resurrection unto eternal life and glory . . . I order something to be given to my servant Abigail Lee . . . this twenty-sixth day of November in ye eleventh year of her Majesty's Reign, Ann, by ye grace

of God of Great Britain, France, and Ireland, Queen, Defender of the Faith, and in ye year of our Lord, 1712.

Deacon Joseph Dewey, born in Westfield in 1714, was a farmer living on West Silver Street. After marrying Beulah Sackett in 1738, they had at least eight children, including Beulah on February 15, 1738; Joseph on March 5, 1740; Benjamin on April 5, 1743; Gad on January 14, 1744; Elijah on November 2, 1746; Beulah on October 12, 1752; Sarah on April 12, 1750; and Mary on January 23, 1753. Benjamin served as a Lieutenant in the American Revolution. In 1773, young Joseph married Hannah Phelps, daughter of Aaron and Rachel (Bagg) Phelps. Sarah died of consumption on October 30, 1799.

John Dewey, born in 1754 to Aaron Dewey and Sarah Noble, was a clothier, and served as selectman. He was one of the Westfield minutemen who answered the call to march to Lexington on April 19, 1775. John Dewey was deeded a fulling mill on Two Mile Brook, adjoining Bagg's grist mill, on April 15, 1789, by Datis Ensign of Chester and Isaac Ensign of Westfield. He married Achsah Clapp on September 16, 1780, and together they had at least seven children, including Sally born on September 2, 1781; John on April 16, 1783; Walter on August 20, 1785; Chester on December 7, 1787; Perez on May 19, 1790; Achsah on May 26, 1795; and Lester on January 12, 1798.

Aaron Dewey, born on Monday, April 28, 1721, married Sarah Noble on Monday, June 12, 1747. Together they had at least nine children including twins Aaron and Sarah born on June 23, 1748; Aaron on January 20, 1750; Aaron on January 15, 1751; John on January 20, 1754; Silas on March 22, 1756; Eunice on March 22, 1758; Silas on January 9, 1761; and Levi on January 28, 1764. Ashbel Dewey, on June 30, 1755, sold to Aaron "the mill pond on Twomile brook, a little west of the old road to Suffield, on both sides of the brook, 40 acres in the whole . . . also all my rights to certain grist mill 1/4 of said mill, etc., 1/4 of the stream on which it stands, near the mouth of Twomile brook."

The Reverend Seth Noble was born in Westfield on April 15, 1743. In June of 1774, he became the minister of the Congregational Church in Maugerville, New Brunswick. At age thirty-two, he married sixteen year old Hannah Barker on November 30, 1775. It was said that the reverend "was too light and frothy in his conversation, did not sustain the gravity of character becoming a minister, would drink a dram with almost anyone who would ask him, laugh and tell improper anecdotes." It was also noted that "he was a good preacher, a most gifted man in prayer, especially on funeral occasions . . . a most excellent singer. He could drink a glass of grog and be jovially merry. When out of the pulpit he ought never to go in, and when in never to go out." He wrote to Aaron Dewey from New Brunswick on May 20, 1776:

> We have had something of a cold season of late, though not colder than it is many times at Westfield. We have about eighteen inches of snow. Mr. Makin died soon after you went away, but nobody since. Jeremiah Howland and Polly Buber were published last Sabbath, and Israel Esty and Salome Burpe. Josiah Whitney is married. It seems to be still as to political affairs. If you could bring a Suffield dishturner, it might be a benefit to the person and to this place. A saddler is much wanted, for there have been near a dozen horses purchased here since you left us. There were sundry opportunities to get a passage from New England here last fall. We have a number of vessels lately come in from over the Bay. We have unanimously signed a paper, to join New England in the national struggle, and are making all possible preparations for war. The fleet and army that went from Boston to Halifax have sailed, we suppose, for England, though they pretended they were going to Quebec.

Adjutant Russell Dewey, brother-in-law, neighbor and friend to General William Shepard, was one of the few men from Westfield to serve throughout the Revolutionary War. Born on August 7, 1754, to Moses and Sarah Dewey, he married Sophia Chapin in 1781, and together they had at least four children, including Sewell born on March 3, 1782; William on June 7, 1784; Sophia on February 9, 1787; and Laura on May 18, 1790. The adjutant wrote in a journal during the ill-fated expedition to capture Quebec in 1776:

Traveled to Washington (January 31, 1776) and tarried in town that day. Feb 1st traveled to Landlord King's in New Lebanon; the 3rd traveled to Landlord Corbins in Albany, had some difficulty, lay at the barber's — viewed the city. Tarried there three days. The 7th, we traveled to Landlord Bryant's in Stillwater; there we heard the Harpsichord and see a negro dance. Feb 15, 1776 we marched on the lake 30 miles with the company, and in the march one span of our horses broke through the ice. It took us an hour to get them out. We made a halt to encamp, it being 20 miles to any house. Sunday, 25th, went to the French church and see them carry on and heard the "Orgain." 27th A post arrived and brot nues that our troops had taken and burnt Boston. March 1, 1776 and 2nd Used the pot together. 4th A fire broke out and burnt up the Armorer's shop and one gun that belonged to our company. 8th we marched on the river 22 miles, it being settled all the way. We came by 11 towns with Churches in them; nothing remarkable except the Captain cursing and swearing at the Lieutenant. Thursday 21st nothing remarkable except hungry men, for we being a fixing for the Small Pox [variolation] might not eat nor drink anything but bread and water - that is we could not get anything else to eat. Sunday March 24th, 1776 it was a cold windy day, and the snow flew and winds was so high, that we were afraid, for fear we should be blowed away, for our preparation for Small Pox brought us so low that we were almost as light as eagles. 26th I began to break out with Small Pox. Saturday, 6th, gun-powder, smoke, fire and balls about these days. Sunday, balls flying in the air. 25th We was alarmed in the night and was ordered to be upon Abraham's Plains immediately, for what we new not, but it was supposed that our men were going to send a "fire ship" in among their shipping, but it being a rainy night we were soon dismissed and nothing was done that night. Friday April 26th There was such a firing that the air was full of balls, some flying one way and some another. Our men being so engaged in firing that they split one of our cannon and killed one of our men.

Timothy Dewey was born to David and Rebecca (Phelps) Dewey on January 24, 1755, and married Asenath Sexton in 1776. Together they had at least eleven children, including Abigail born on October 3, 1777; Clarissa on January 4, 1779; Sally on October 28, 1781; Charles on April 22, 1784; Timothy on June 24, 1786; John on November 24, 1790; Submit on November 22, 1791; Eliakim on August 12, 1794; Roland on December 15, 1795; Daniel on March 1, 1801; and Thomas in 1803.

The Dewey family line continues today. Bob Dewey is a member of the Westfield Historical Commission, and has made the Old Burying Ground a personal project. With perseverance, he was able to uncover the remnants of a headstone of one of his ancestors. He recreated the original design, paying close attention to the details, and had the stone replaced with a new granite version, which now stands in the old burying ground on Mechanic Street.

CORNET
THOMAS DEW
EY DYED APRIL
27TH ANO 1690 IN
THE 52 YEARE OF
HIS AGE

Carved by George Griswold

MRS
CONSTANT
DEWEY DYED
ON APR THE
27 1702 AGED
58 YEAR CORT
THO DEWEY
WIFE

Carved by Joseph Nash

In Memory of
Mrs Sarah
Wife of
Lieut Moses
Dewey who
died april 7 1762
in her 47 Year

Time was like thee
I life passed
& time will be
when thou shalt rest

Carved by Joseph Williston

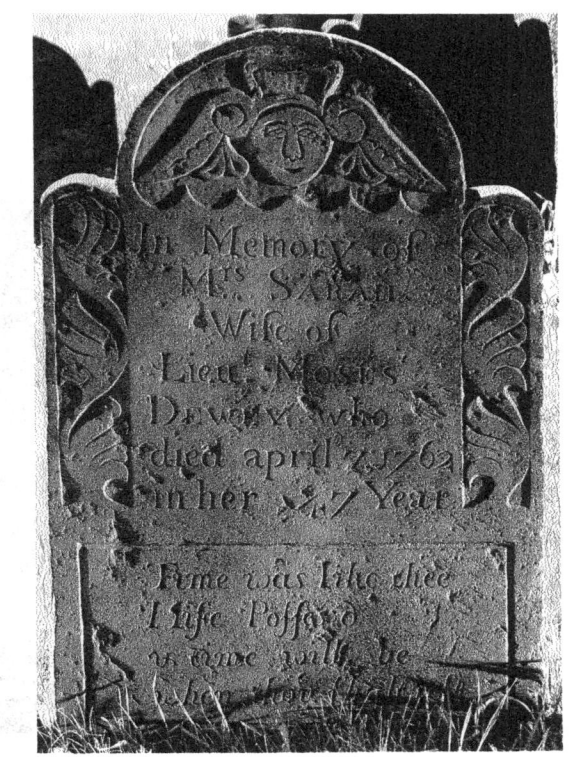

In memory of
Mr Adijah
Dewey who
died January
31 1753 AE 59

Carved by Nathaniel Phelps

In memory of
Perez son of
Mr John & Mrs
Acksah Dewey
who died
17th Augt 1790
Aged 15 months

Carved by John Ely

Aaron Son
of Mr Aaron & Mrs
Sarah Dewey
who died Nov
13th 1749 in ye 9th
Year of his Age

In Memory of
Mr Aaron
Dewey who
died June ye 11th
1768 in ye 48th
Year of his
Age

Carved by Aaron Bliss

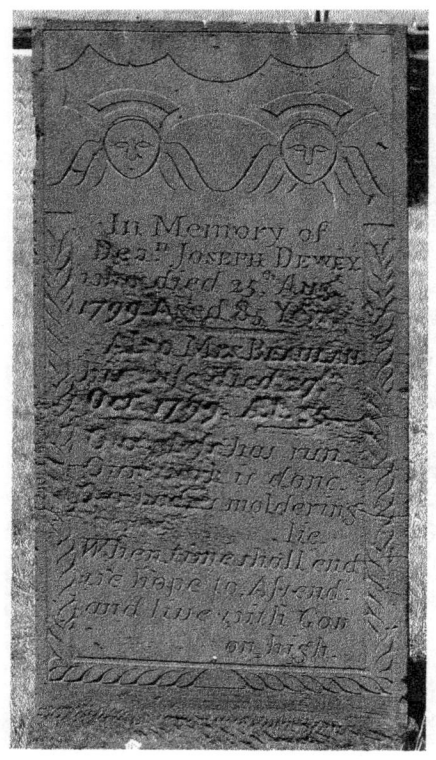

In memory of
Deacn Joseph Dewey
who died 25th Augst
1799 Aged 85 Years
Also Mrs Beulah
his wife who died 27th
Oct 1769 AEt 55

Our glass has run,
Our work is done,
Our bodies mouldering lie.
When time shall end,
we hope to ascend,
and live with God
on high.

Carved by John Ely

*Timothy Dewey
died Feb 19 1839
Aged 84.
Asenath Dewey
wife of
Timothy Dewey
died Jan 26th 1836
Aged 78*

Carved by G. Viets

IN MEMORY OF
MR DAVID DEWEY
WHO DIED JANY 5TH 1813
IN THE 88 YEAR OF HIS AGE
ALSO HIS WIFE REBECAH
DEWEY WHO DIED THE 25TH OF
APRIL 1812 IN HER 80TH YEAR

THESE DIED TOGETHER
HAPPY IN UNION
UNDIVORCED BY DEATH

ORIGINAL STONE
REPLACED IN 2008
R G DEWEY

This granite headstone is a replica of the original marble headstone.
Replacement is an effective method of preserving genealogical data in an
historic burying ground.

The Nobles

With Noble Hospital being a landmark in Westfield today, it can come as no surprise that the Noble family has a long and illustrious history here. Thomas Noble, born in England in 1632, married Hannah Warriner on November 1, 1660, and together they had at least ten children including Mark; John born on March 6, 1662; Hannah on February 24, 1664; Thomas on January 14, 1666; Matthew in 1668; Elizabeth on February 9, 1673; Luke on July 15, 1675; James on October 1, 1677; Mary on June 29, 1680; and Rebecca on January 4, 1683. Thomas and Hannah had ninety-six grandchildren, establishing the Noble name for years to come in Westfield. He was granted permission to build a saw mill on the west side of the Great River in 1664, while living in Springfield. Thomas received land grants in 1666, located about two and a half miles east of Westfield center. By 1667, he was deeply in debt to John Pynchon's store and was forced to sign over his house and all lands except for a grant near Windsor, Connecticut, to Pynchon. By January 21, 1669, Thomas was recorded attending a town meeting in Warronoco, one of the many spelling variations for early Westfield. On April 7, 1674, he was sworn in as the local constable. During King Philip's War in 1675, the local Indian called Greylock was a pesky visitor, harassing the family, and Thomas was persuaded to move them to the center of town, into the safety of the forted area. Following Thomas' death, Hannah married Deacon Medad Pomeroy, who besides being deacon was also a blacksmith, town clerk, and state representative between 1677 and 1692.

The oldest surviving gravestone in Westfield honors Abigail, the wife of John, who died in 1683 at the age of 20, just four days after the birth of her first and only son. She was born to John and Abigail Sackett on December 1, 1663.

Matthew Noble married Hannah Dewey on December 10, 1690, and together they had at least eight children including Joseph born on October 8, 1691; Hezekiah on May 14, 1694; Matthew on September 19, 1698; Solomon on December 23, 1700; Elisha on February 9, 1702; Obediah on October 19, 1705; Hannah on October 11, 1707; and Rhoda on April 17, 1717. He was involved in a lawsuit on February 27, 1696, when he was summoned to appear in court in a "Plea of Trespass brought by John Gun for felling and taking away Pine Trees of said Guns ground granted him by the Towne for turpentine." Matthew settled a town in the Berkshires named Nobletown in his honor. Following the defeat of the British at Saratoga in 1777, the Hessian Major General Baron von Riedesel's family was marched through the area. One of his officers wrote in his journal that they were forced to stay in "the wretched village of Nobletown" overnight. When Robert Noble, a leader of the rent agitators in the "anti-rent war" in New York, was forced back to Massachusetts by the Albany 46th Royal Infantry in 1766, the town was renamed Hillsdale. Matthew was also credited with being the first English settler to reach the current town of Sheffield, Massachusetts, after crossing "hideous howling wilderness" from Westfield in 1725. The town was surveyed by Captain John Ashley, Ebenezer Pomeroy, and Thomas Ingersoll.

Ensign Matthew Noble, an ancestor of Nancy Reagan, born to Matthew and Hannah (Dewey) Noble on September 19, 1698, married Joanna Stebbins of Springfield on May 31, 1720. Together they had at least eight children including Bethia born on April 20, 1721; Joanna on December 3, 1722; Constantine on October 8, 1725; Gideon on March 6, 1728; Rhoda on August 28, 1730; Rhoda on August 28, 1732; Matthew on July 27, 1736; and Paul on January 14, 1740. In 1745, Ensign Noble was listed as a tanner, in 1754 as a saddler, and in 1759 as a cordwainer. On July 25, 1766, he married Mercy Day of West Springfield. Matthew was selectman, moderator of the town meeting, and representative to the General Court.

Samuel Noble died of pleurisy at age fifty-one on November 4, 1773. He was chosen selectman in 1760 and 1761. Reverend Ballantine wrote "Visited Sergeant Noble, prayed. Died while I was there. Aged 51, was an hearty, strong man. He was at the Ordination last week, was taken ill in the night after. Proper means were neglected in the beginning, for want of a skillful Physician. The distemper which was a pleurisy in the Breast prevailed. He was one of the Selectmen, hath been chosen several times into that Office. He made a profession of Religion & was under the watch of the church, had some his children baptized, joined with the Separates, very rarely met with us for worship."

Matthew Noble, son of Matthew and Joanna (Stebbins) Noble born on July 27, 1736, became a tanner and saddler in Westfield, serving as a second lieutenant in the Revolutionary War in Captain Mosely's company. On November 14, 1758, he married Lydia Eager, and together they had at least eleven children, including Eager born on May 15, 1760; Sally on April 29, 1762; Lydia on August 16, 1764; William on December 6, 1765; William on March 28, 1768; Dorothy on March 10, 1770; Clarissa on September 13, 1773; John on August 10, 1776; Charles on August 17, 1778; Henry on December 17, 1781; and Pamela on January 5, 1784.

Lieutenant Stephen Noble, born on April 16, 1727, to Deacon Thomas and Sarah (Root), married Ruth Church on March 7, 1753. Together they had at least eight children, including Louisa born on June 5, 1754; Ruth on June 1, 1756; Bildad on May 13, 1759; Aaron on March 13, 1761; Stephen on April 7, 1765; Lois on June 1, 1767; Eunice on April 30, 1770; and Lucinda on January 27, 1774. Stephen served in the Continental Army for eight months in 1777. He is listed as being short in stature, running his father's farm, and working as an innkeeper.

HERE
LYETH THE
BODY OF ABIG
AIL THE WIFE OF
JOHN NOBLE WHO
DIED JULY 3D ANO
1683 IN YE 20TH YEAR
OF HER AGE

Carved by George Griswold

This is the earliest known gravestone in the old burying ground on Mechanic Street.

Here Lies ye
Body of Mrs
Bethiah ye wife
of Mr Silas
Noble who
died May ye
5th 1763 in
ye 24th Year
of her Age

Carved by Thomas Spelman

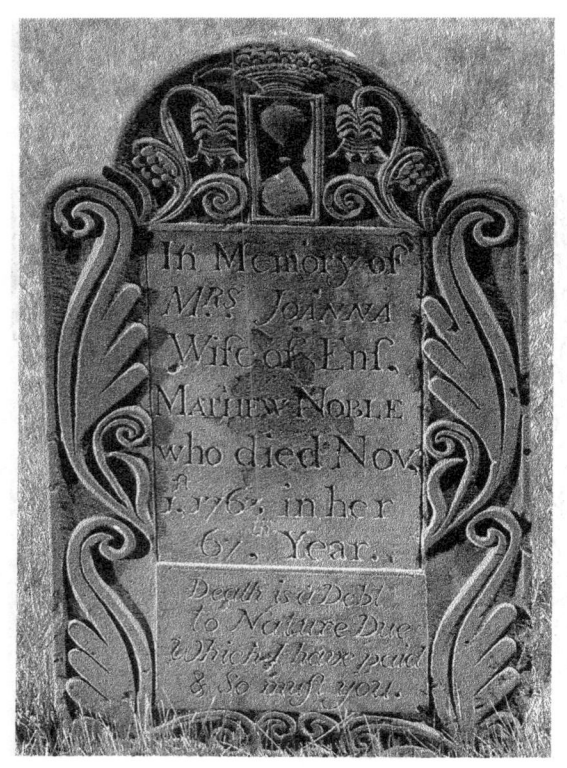

In Memory of
Mrs Joanna
Wife of Ens
Matthew Noble
who died Nov
1st 1763 in her
67th Year

Death is a debt
to Nature Due
Which I have paid
& so must you

Carved by Ezra Stebbins

In Memory of
Lt Stephen Noble
Who died April 2d 1791
In ye 64 year of his
Age

My flesh shall slumber
in the Ground
till the last trumpets
Joyful Sound
then burst the Chains
with sweet Surprise
& in my Saviour's
Image rise

Carved by Stebbins shop

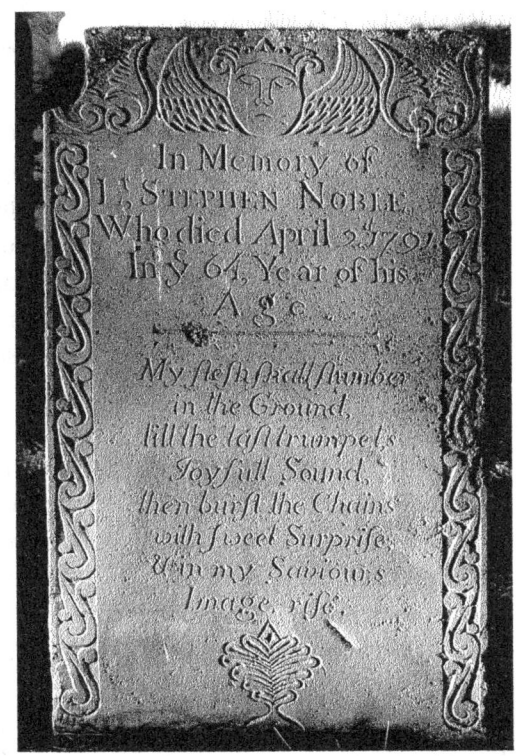

The Moselys

The Mosely family arrived in Westfield in 1666, settling in the South Meadow. Being an important member of Westfield society meant that the Mosely daughters were able to marry into the best families in the area. Colonel David Mosely's daughters took advantage of their high status and all married well. Margaret married John Ingersoll, who helped develop the Constitution of Massachusetts in 1780. Mercy married the Honorable John Phelps, a local lawyer who built an extensive practice after graduating from Yale in 1759. Rhoda married Dr. Charles Mather, a prominent physician of Hartford, Connecticut, a Yale graduate of 1763, and a descendant of Cotton Mather's brother. Grace married the Honorable Samuel Mather, cousin to her sister's husband, a well-known statesman, and also a graduate of Yale in 1758.

John Mosely, son of John and Mary (Newberry) Mosely, was born in Windsor, Connecticut, on August 21, 1678 and married Hannah Grant on April 7, 1712. They had at least one child, Margaret, born on June 2, 1714. In 1682, John's father tried to keep the town from building a lane next to his property by presenting a petition to the Massachusetts General Court. The church intervened, accusing him of breaking three of the Ten Commandments. According to the church, John broke the eighth commandment by relying on the town instead of his own labors, the ninth by filing a false claim against the town of Westfield, and the tenth by attempting to keep the town from building the lane.

David Mosely, son of Joseph and Abigail (Root) Mosely, was born on February 9, 1705, and married Margaret Dewey. Together they had at least six children, including Margaret born on November 15, 1730; Hannah on March 20, 1733;

David on March 7, 1735; Grace on May 16, 1739; Mercy on July 26, 1742; and Rhoda on May 24, 1745. On December 9, 1754, David was an assessor in Westfield, along with Israel Ashley and William Sacket, when they certified that there were fifteen male and four female Negro slaves living in Westfield. When David died in January, 1768, Reverend Ballantine wrote, "Preached a funeral sermon for David Mosely, Esquire, Aged 63, in the meeting House, followed him to the Grave, a great many people."

David, son of David and Margaret (Dewey) Mosely, was born on March 7, 1735, and married Lydia Gay and together they had at least 10 children including David born on December 27, 1762; William on April 26, 1764; Lydia on March 14, 1766; Mary on March 25, 1768; Elijah on April 2, 1770; Frances on July 24, 1772; Jeremiah on January 20, 1777; Nancy on April 22, 1779; Betsey on August 31, 1781; and Synthia on August 30, 1783.

Bohan King, son of Reuben and Sarah (Mosely) King, lived on Elm Street, and served as a hatter's apprentice for six years in Northampton before opening his own hattery in Westfield in 1769. He married Thankful Taylor on January 3, 1771. During the Revolutionary War, he was the constable, sending three Tories to jail in Northampton for refusing to serve as soldiers in 1777. He was elected to the second Committee of Correspondence and Safety on December 28, 1775.

Colonel James Taylor, born in 1745, married Mary Moseley, and together they had at least five children. They were Clarissa, born in 1772, Roland in 1774, James in 1777, Julia in 1786, and Polly in 1790. The Reverend James Taylor was a Trustee of Amherst College from 1821 until his death in 1831. Graduating from Williams College in 1803, he studied theology under the Reverend John Taylor of Deerfield, marrying his eldest daughter, Elizabeth, on July 22, 1807.

Noah Madsly
Son to john
Madsly Died
May 24 1735
Aged 2 year

In
Memory of Qrs
John Mosely
Who died Augst
6th 1752 aged
74 years

Carved by Nathaniel Phelps

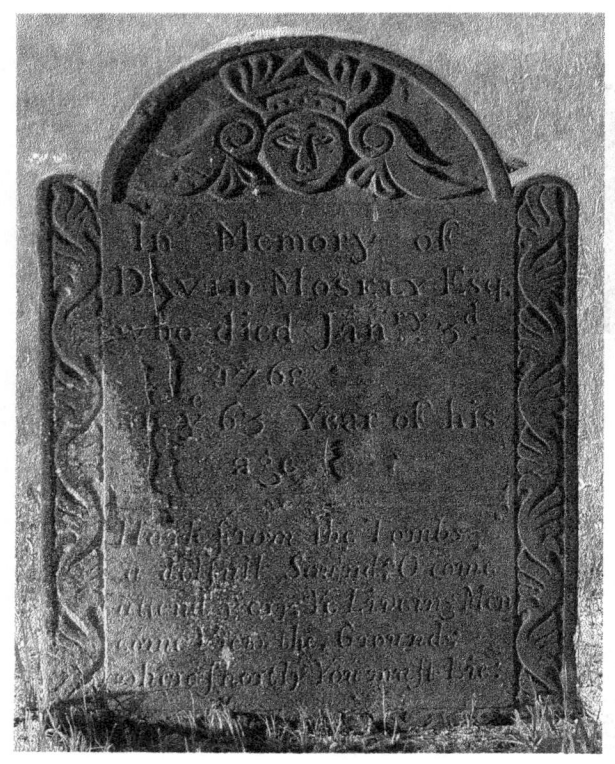

In Memory of
David Mosely Esq
who died Janry 3d
1768
in ye 63 year of his
age

Hark from the Tombs
a dolfull sound O come
attend ye cry, ye Liveing Men
come view the Ground
where shortly You must Lie

Carved by Joseph Williston

In Memory of
Mrs Margaret
wife of
David Mosely
Esq
who died Janry 4th
1762 in her
56th Year

Carved by Joseph Williston

Underneath this stone lies
Mouldering to dust the
Once amiable & Very
Desirable Man
Mr Daniel Mosely
who died March ye 6th
1777 Aged 64 Years

The Grave hath Eloquence
it lectures to each
Louder in silence
than Divines can Preach

Carved by Ezra Stebbins

In Memory of
Mrs Hannah
wife of
Qut Master
John Mosely
who died april 27th
1763 in ye   Year
of her age

Reader remember
Death & Eternity

Carved by Joseph Williston

The Sackets

John Sacket was the first birth recorded in Cambridge, Massachusetts, being born in 1632. His parents, Simon and Isabel (Pearce) Sackett, came from the Isle of Ely in England. John dropped the last 't' in his surname, separating him from the rest of his relatives at the time. John moved to Springfield from Cambridge in 1653 with his brother Simon, settling in Chicopee, and then removed to Northampton. On November 23, 1659, he married Abigail Hannum, and together they had at least nine children, including John born in 1660, William in 1662, Abigail in 1663, Mary in 1665, Hannah in 1669, Mary in 1672, Samuel in 1674, Elizabeth in 1677, and Abigail in 1683. During this time he established himself as a successful farmer and Indian trader; he was fined forty shillings on March 7, 1661, for selling strong drink to the Indians. The family moved to Westfield in 1667, onto land purchased from Deacon Samuel Chapin, which subsequently became known as Sacket's Meadows.

On October 27, 1675, Sacket's house and barn were burned and his cattle driven off his land during an Indian raid in King Philip's War. Brothers Thomas, Jedediah, and Jonah Dewey brought a lawsuit against John Sacket, Samuel Taylor, a blacksmith on South Street, Joseph Pomeroy, and Nathaniel Williams for building a mill further up the brook from their own, disrupting essential water flow. It was brought in the courts in Northampton, appealed to the General Court, and finally settled in the court in Springfield in the autumn of 1685, finding that the Deweys were the sole proprietors of that section of stream. As part of the settlement, the Deweys spent nine days helping to dismantle Sacket's dam and move the offending mill to another location. Between 1672 and 1693, John served numerous terms as selectman and constable in Westfield. On January 14, 1693, he married Sarah Stuart, widow of John Stuart of Springfield. Their daughter was reportedly taken captive by the Indians, and later married a chief in northern New York. Sacket finally sold his land in "Chicuppi field" for five pounds on June 4, 1703, to William Scott of Springfield.

John Sacket, born on November 4, 1660, married Deborah Filley on December 1, 1686. Together they had at least six children, including John born on March 3, 1688, Abigail on October 16, 1690, Daniel on August 14, 1693, David on July 7, 1696, Benjamin on October 31, 1698, and Deborah on November 16, 1701.

William Sacket was born on April 12, 1662 in Northampton to John and Abigail (Hannum) Sacket. On December 26, 1687 William married Sarah Crain. He married Hannah Graves on November 27, 1689. Together they had at least two children, including Joseph born on July 25, 1690, and Jonathan on March 20, 1696. Coming home from a wedding, William drowned in the Connecticut River on March 28, 1700. In a meeting on February 11, 1667, it was "ordered that a convenient gate easy and handy shutting & opening shall . . . be set over the brook from Sackets house further into the meadow . . . whoever shall leave open or not shut the gate shall pay 5s to the use of the proprietors."

Daniel Sacket, born on August 14, 1693, married Mary Weller. Together they had at least ten children including Margaret born on December 4, 1732, Daniel on March 6, 1733, Ozem on January 24, 1735, Mary on November 21, 1738, Ann on February 28, 1740, Moses on November 29, 1743, Israel on February 10, 1745, twins Asher and Gad on April 17, 1748, and Abner on October 11, 1751. Daniel served as a sentinel in Captain Adgat Dewey's troop of horse in 1723. He also served under Captain Hezekiah Noble and Captain John Ashley.

Moses Sacket, born on November 29, 1743, married Eunice Caldwell on November 1, 1770. Together they had at least eleven children, including Philana born on June 23, 1771; Olive on September 4, 1773; Eunice on March 19, 1775; Martin on December 23, 1776; Olive on August 3, 1779; John on March 30, 1781; Heman on September 30, 1783; Frances on May 26, 1786; Erastus on October 16, 1790; Israel on September 6, 1792; and Roxana on December 22, 1795.

Adnah Sacket, born to Isaac and Elizabeth (Shepard) Sacket on December 5, 1745, married Jerusha Pomeroy on October 13, 1767. Adnah was commissioned First Lieutenant on April 22, 1776, in Captain Daniel Sackett's company. Jerusha's father, Lieutenant Daniel Pomeroy of Northampton, was killed at the battle of Lake George on September 8, 1755. Her uncle, General Seth Pomeroy, served during the Revolutionary War, distinguishing himself at the battle of Bunker Hill. Adnah was an innkeeper in Westfield, living on a farm and raising horses. Together they had at least eight children, including Jerusha born on May 27, 1769; John on January 27, 1771; Charlotte on May 27, 1773; Isaac in 1777, George in 1779, Israel in 1781, Olive in 1783, and Lydia in 1785. On May 4, 1790, Adnah married Mercy Bush.

Moses Sackett, born on December 3, 1766, married Tryphena Hiscock on December 24, 1795. Together they had at least twelve children, including Tryphena born on March 17, 1797; Moses on August 11, 1798; Levi on April 3, 1800; Tryphosa on July 26, 1801; Walter in 1803; Persis on March 5, 1805; William on April 19, 1807; Martin on February 7, 1809; Serepta on May 16, 1811; Nancy on May 4, 1813; Noah on February 11, 1815; and Laura on June 30, 1817.

John Sacket, born on March 30, 1781, married Rachel Morse on November 26, 1807. Together they had at least eight children, including William born on September 25, 1808; Anna on March 28, 1812; Orren on October 26, 1814; Roxana on January 19, 1819; Cordelia on January 22, 1821; Clarissa on July 24, 1826; Melissa on June 11, 1828; and Eunice on July 1, 1810.

In the journal of the Reverend John Ballantine on November 30, 1760, he wrote "James Stevenson prayers for his child burnt. William Sackett & Wife, thanks for recovery from child bearing." On January 26, 1759, "Caesar, William Sacketts negro died, how many warnings have youth, how inexcusable if they neglect to prepare on presumption that they will live to be old, earthly enjoyment uncertain."

ABIGAIL THE
WIFE OF JOHN
SACKET SHEE DYED
OCTO THE 10TH DAY
ANO 1690 AGED
49 YEARS

Carved by George Griswold

In Memory of
Mr Adnah Sacket
who died
26th April 1813
Aged 66 Years

Carved by John Ely

In Memory of
Mrs Jerusha wife of
Lt Adnah Sacket
who died Dec 10
1789 aged 41 years

The wintry blast of death
kills not the buds of virtue
no they spread
beneath the heavenly beam
of brighter suns
thro endless ages to higher
Powers

Carved by Stebbins shop

Sacred to the Memory
of Mrs Mercy, wife of
Lt Adnah Sacket
who Died April 20 1791
In ye 32 Year of her
Age
& was interd in this
Grave with 2 infant
Children

Carved by Stebbins shop

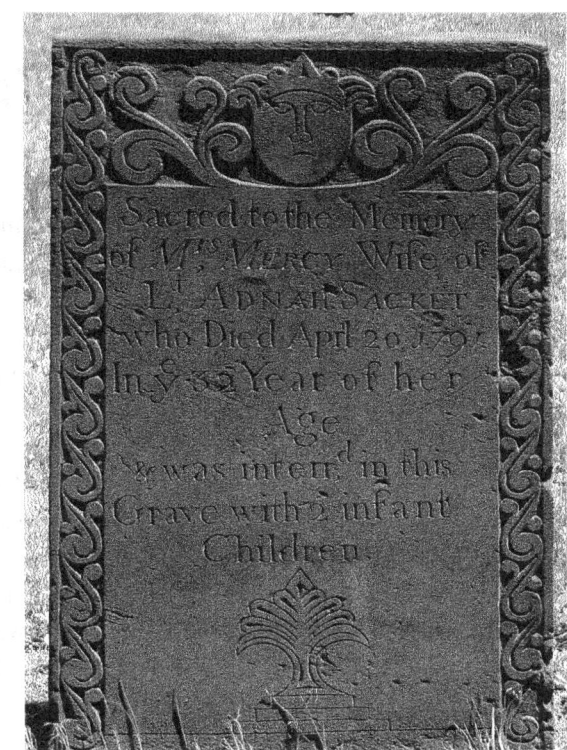

The Fowlers

Samuel Fowler, born on January 1, 1710, to Samuel Fowler and Mercy Root, married Naomi Noble on May 8, 1734. Settling in the south of Westfield in an area called Poverty Plains, now the town of Southwick, the Fowlers had at least 10 children, including Eunice; Silas born on May 23, 1735; Abner on November 6, 1737; Naomi on December 12, 1739; Ruth on March 22, 1741; Mercy on August 20, 1744; Samuel on September 5, 1747; Eleanor on September 18, 1752; Lucy on September 1, 1758; and Noble on January 10, 1763.

Bildad Fowler studied under Reverend Ballantine, graduating from college in 1773. When summoned to join the patriotic army in 1777 he refused, opting instead to go to jail in Northampton. Twenty-four hours later he was released on condition that he join the army, which he did and served faithfully, eventually being elected selectman in Westfield.

James Fowler was one of the original fire wardens chosen at the April town meeting in 1817, along with Amos Fowler, Colonel Horace Noble, Dr. William Atwater, Erastus Grant, Captain Charles Douglas, Captain John Mather, and Elijah Bates. A suction fire engine known as "The Deluge" was purchased in 1832 for $300, serving the town until it was lost in the canal.

In Memory of
Mr. Samuel Fowler
who died Jany 4th
AD 1771
In the 59th Year
of his Age

So brittle is the state of man
So soon it doth decay
So all the glory of this world
Must pass and fade away

Carved by Nathaniel Phelps

In Memory of
Mrs Mercy
Fowler
who died
Janry 6th 1743
in her 24th Year

A Law Eternal
does decree
That all things born
Shall Mortal be

Carved by Joseph Williston
(backdated)

EDWARD
GRISWOLD
SON OF GEORGE
AND MARY GRIS-
WOLD: HE DIED
MAY 30 1688
AGED 27 YEARS

Carved by George Griswold

Edward Griswold was born in Windsor, Connecticut in 1660, to George, a gravestone carver from England, and Mary Holcomb of Dorcester, Massachusetts. He moved to Westfield and married Abigail Williams on November 3, 1681. They had two children, Edward on December 16, 1682 and Abigail on August 3, 1685. Edward was admitted to the church in Westfield in 1685.

How They Died

From the records of the First Church:

On August 8, 1747, Abel Drake killd by ye overturning a Cart of Hay in a brook. There was an earthquake on the 15th.

Edward Bancroft subject to an Epilepsy, and ye Day of His Death, something inclined to a fit, but so well as to be able to go about Town, was abroad in ye evening, went to tend his Hogs, staying longer yn usual, the Family going to look after him, found him dead in the Sty.

Noah Pixly killed by Indians, New Hampton, walking in ye street ab't 10 o'clock morn ab't mile from meeting house.

May 26, 1758 Israel Noble drowned getting logs in the Great River.

April 28, 1765, Mr. Ashbel Dewey--ye last of his Father's Children, who all died of Consumption.

July 11, 1784, a delirious transient woman whose name and place of abode were unknown 70 years.

September 24, 1784, Charles Ensign drowned, aged 1 year seven months.

According to Isaac Knapp, "In the year 1803 (Westfield) was visited with distressing sickness. There being then no settled Minister, the records were not accurately kept. It appears, after taking great pains to make inquiry, that seventy-six died in the course of this year. The dysantery prevailed from about the middle of July til October. Fifty died of this disorder."

March 1804, James Mowit perished in a snowstorm the fore part of this month 50 years.

December 1, 1805, Festus Paulk (Polk) 34 years, his wife 36 years, his son 3 years six months, his daughter 1 year six months, all were consumed by fire between the hours of ten and eleven o'clock at night together with the grist & saw mills near Capt. Moses Dewey's house.

Gauzy Williams fought in the War of 1812. He was scalped by Indians and left for dead, but was able to use some of his clothes to bind the wound, and made it back home alive. While cutting wood one day the old wound opened and "let out his brains and he died."

December 3, 1813, Orin Granger killed by the blowing up of a powder mill 20 years.

September 29, 1827, the wife of Robert Bush murdered by her husband 36 years.

The Old Burying Ground

The Old Burying Ground was established on April 27, 1668, just west of the meetinghouse, and is one of the oldest remaining in its original location in the United States. One of the duties of the early selectmen was to "take care that the burying place be cleared of brush." John Bancroft was granted use of the burying ground for pasturing livestock for thirty years in February of 1703. In March of 1710, John Lee 2nd was chosen to dig graves in the Old Burying Ground at a rate of three shillings apiece. The selectmen were responsible for funerals paid at the town expense. The town meeting in May of 1778 voted on a motion that "the burying place be enclosed by a good fence" and not be used as a pasture. When Westfield acquired the William Phillips property in 1827, the size of the burying grounds almost doubled. The original entrance on Main Street was moved to the current position on Mechanic Street in 1834. For years, a wooden fence surrounded the old burying ground until in 1872, the town paid a little over five hundred dollars for a wrought iron fence, selling off the old wooden pieces for twenty dollars. A fancy gate cost almost as much as the whole fence surrounding the cemetery, for which the town paid about three hundred and sixty dollars in 1894. Maintaining the old yard has been a concern of the town for many years. In 1904, Daniel Leonard was paid nine dollars and fifty cents for repairing headstones. The last recorded burial was in 1934, when Mary Noble Fox was laid to rest there.

Thomas Ingersoll was born in Westfield on March 28, 1668, and married Sarah Ashley on July 22, 1692. Together they had at least five children including Thomas born on November 27, 1692; Moses on February 10, 1694; Miriam on June 4, 1697; David on September 30, 1699; and Eleanor on March 12, 1704. Sarah died in 1704, and Thomas married two more times, but had no more children. On January 21, 1708, he wed Abigail Dickinson of Springfield, and on May 17, 1720, he married Ruth Child of Watertown.

His son Esquire Thomas inherited "Ingersoll Place," being a magistrate in Westfield appointed by King George. The homestead was fortified in case of Indian attack, and was frequently used for that purpose. He married Sarah, daughter of Abijah Dewey, in 1715. Esquire Thomas was later responsible for ending the life of the Indian called Greylock, "a cruel and cunning savage murderer," who was attempting to scalp Thomas's wife, Sarah. Thomas was elected selectman twelve times and served as representative for Westfield at the General Court in Boston. He helped push the boundaries of Westfield, acquiring territory in present-day Russell and Montgomery. Together Thomas and Sarah had at least eight children, including Jonathan born on January 24, 1715; Daniel on May 26, 1718; Sarah on January 27, 1720; Miriam on November 4, 1723; Margaret on February 1, 1728; John on February 26, 1731; Mary on November 16, 1733; and Ann on June 21, 1737, who married Colonel Sluman of the British Army.

Captain Jonathan Ingersoll, born January 24, 1716, to Esquire Thomas and Sarah (Dewey) Ingersoll, married Eunice Mosely on November 15, 1738. He died at the Battle of Lake George, along with Noah Ashley and Richard Campbell from Westfield, on September 8, 1755, during the French and Indian War. His aunt Hester, born to John and Abigail Ingersoll on September 9, 1665, enjoyed an interesting life. In 1684, she married William Gurley of Northampton, who came from Inverness, Scotland, was raised by the Reverend Solomon Stoddard, and drowned in the Connecticut River at age twenty-two, leaving behind a one week old son, Samuel. One of Samuel's descendants who bore his name became the chaplain of the American Congress.

Hester later married Benoni Jones on January 23, 1689, and together they had four children including Jonathan born on January 4, 1695; Benjamin in 1696, Ebenezer on November 12, 1698; and Jonathan on March 3, 1703. On May 13, 1704, just a few weeks after the attack to the north known as the Deerfield Massacre, a group of French and Indians attacked Pascommuck, a tiny village of thirty-three people in five families located in current-day Easthampton. The only fortified house was that of Benoni Jones, which the marauders immediately burned. When Patience Webb looked out the window to see what was happening, she was shot in the face and killed, causing the rest of the village to surrender. Nineteen villagers were killed, including Benoni and two of his children, eight escaped, and six were taken captive. Hannah, the wife of Benjamin Jones, was scalped and left for dead on the top of Pomeroy Mountain, but was rescued and later recovered, living to the age of eighty. Before they could reach Canada, three of the captives escaped. Hester survived the long treacherous trek to Canada, but died on November 27, 1705, in Montreal.

The Reverend Noah Atwater was born on January 3, 1752, to Jacob and Miriam (Ives) Atwater of New Haven, Connecticut. He graduated from Yale in 1774, and then worked as a butler for two years, followed by tutoring responsibilities for three years. Once he obtained his preaching license in New Haven on May 27, 1778, he was able to practice in Westfield in early 1778. A smallpox outbreak that year prevented him from staying, but he returned in 1781 to be ordained as their minister on November twenty-first, and preached there for twenty years. He married Rachel Lyman, daughter of Captain William Lyman of Northampton, in 1783, and together they had a son, William, born on January 30, 1786, who graduated from Yale in 1807. When Rachel died on September 16, 1787, Noah married Anna Lockwood of Milford, Connecticut.

Ensign Stephen Kellogg, born on April 9, 1668, to Joseph and Abigail (Terry) Kellogg in Hadley, Massachusetts, married Lydia Beldon (Belding) on May 8, 1684. Moving to Westfield in 1697, his occupation is listed as a weaver. Together they had at least eleven children including Stephen, Amos, Lydia, Moses, Abigail, Daniel, Ephraim, Mercy, Noah, Silas, and Aaron.

Captain Samuel Kellogg was born on April 1, 1687, to John and Sarah (Moody) Kellogg in Hadley. At a town meeting in 1713, Kellogg was granted money to build a bridge over Two Mile Brook. In early 1714, Kellogg, along with Captain Joseph Maudsley and Samuel Bishop, was given the "liberty to build a sawmill and grist mill at ye half mile fall and they are to have the liberty of the stream no longer than they keep a mill or mills in repair for ye use of ye town." On July 8, 1714, he married his cousin Mary Ashley, and together they had at least eight children including Josiah born on December 11, 1715; Samuel on November 9, 1717; David on May 30, 1721, who served in the expedition to annex Canada under General Amherst; Seth on May 15, 1723; twin daughters on January 19, 1724, who did not live a day; a son on January 25, 1725, who died the same day; and John on July 5, 1727. Captain Samuel married Mary's sister, also his cousin, on June 3, 1728. Together they had at least four children including Justus on March 17, 1729; Mary on October 24, 1730; Shem on January 1, 1732; and Sarah on July 25, 1734.

Edward Martindale was born on February 16, 1690. In his will he says "Being weak and under difficult Circumstances of Body, but of perfect mind and memory Thanks be given to God for the same . . . my body I recommend to the earth to be buried in a Decent Christian burial at the Discretion of my Christian friends and Relations nothing doubting that at the Resurection I shall receive the same by the mighty power of God." Edward married Ruth Smead in Deerfield, Massachusetts, on May 4, 1721. Together they had at least ten children including Esther born on April 22, 1722; Gershom in 1724; Sarah on November 29, 1726; Zadock on December 20, 1728; Lemuel on October 20, 1730;

Ebenezer on March 12, 1733; Esther on October 12, 1734; Elisha on February 26, 1736; Edward on February 7, 1740; and Thankful on February 22, 1744. On July 21, 1731, Edward, identified as a 'clothier,' purchased twenty acres of land with a house, barn, and orchard for two hundred pounds from Ebenezer Fletcher, a local physician. On July 19, 1733, he purchased land on East Mountain from Joseph Pixley for forty pounds.

John Bancroft was born on July 16, 1755, to Captain John and Mercy (Ashley) Bancroft, and married Elizabeth Holcomb on October 1, 1778. That was the year that his father built the first brick house in Westfield. Together they had at least eight children including Hannah born on June 26, 1780; Mercy on October 5, 1782; John on August 29, 1783; Edward on August 27, 1785; Elizabeth on November 8, 1787; Daniel on August 30, 1788; Polly on December 3, 1791; and Royal on September 1, 1794. Bancroft was placed under house arrest during the Revolution for aiding British troops.

> The Committee of Correspondence, Inspection, and Safety, of the town of Westfield, having heretofore had many complaints of the inimical temper and disposition of Captain John Bancroft, of said Westfield, towards the grand struggle for the preservation of American liberty . . . received into his house, fed, and refreshed the notorious Captain McKay . . . on his escape . . . from Hartford, and endeavor to get through the woods to Quebeck, there to join the Ministerial butchers, to cut the throats of our brethren in Canada . . . by his own confession . . . does not fairly prove that the said Captain John Bancroft is an enemy to American liberty? It passed in the affirmative. Resolved, unanimously, that the said John ought to be held up to publick view as an enemy to American Liberty.

The first Committee of Correspondence, Inspection, and Safety consisted of some of the most influential and prominent men of the town, including Dr. Samuel Mather, Colonel John Mosely, Captain William Shepard, Eldad Taylor Esq., Colonel Elisha Parks, Daniel Mosely, Daniel Fowler, Captain David Mosely, Deacon Joseph Root, William Sackett, Samuel Fowler, Lieutenant John Shepard Jr., and John Phelps.

Doctor Samuel Mather was born to Doctor Samuel and Mary (Holcomb) Mather of Northampton on June 10, 1737. He graduated from Yale in 1756, studied medicine under his father's tutelage, and began practicing physic and surgery in Westfield in 1759. Becoming a skilled physician, he soon acquired a large practice, and married Grace Moseley in 1761. Shortly thereafter, King George III commissioned him as Justice of the Peace in Westfield, and he served as town clerk and treasurer, and was elected representative. He was appointed senator, and judge of the County Court, just in time for Shays' Rebellion. Following the attack on the Springfield Armory in 1787, Judge Mather became Doctor Mather, dressing the wounds of the rebels injured during the uprising. Doctor Samuel and Grace Mather had at least nine children, including Grace born on February 10, 1763; Samuel on December 13, 1764; Lucy on January 20, 1767; Roland on January 15, 1769; Erastus on October 11, 1770; Sophia on October 11, 1772; John on February 27, 1776; Cynthia on January 25, 1777; and Thomas on September 27, 1780.

Ebenezer Bush, born on July 24, 1687, to Samuel and Mary (Goodenow) Bush, married Mary Taylor in July of 1710. Together they had at least seven children including Lucy born on March 5, 1711; Ebenezer on June 2, 1713; Huldah on February 2, 1715; Zachariah on November 11, 1718; David on December 7, 1721; Aaron on May 26, 1725; and Hannah on June 24, 1729. On November 30, 1752, Ebenezer married Thankful Hitchcock. Silas, son of Zachariah and Mary Ann (Loomis) Bush, was born on March 6, 1748, and married Anne Weller on August 23, 1770. During the

Revolutionary War, Silas was listed as a Sergeant in Captain Daniel Sacket's company, serving in Colonel John Moseley's regiment from October 21, 1776, to November 17, 1776. On the expedition to Saratoga he served in Captain David Mosely's company from September 21, 1777, to October 17, 1777. Aaron Bush, born in 1725 to Ebenezer and Mary (Taylor) Bush, married Mary Ashley, daughter of David, on August 28, 1750. Together they had at least one child, Gideon born on December 1, 1750.

In the late 1600s, a large number of Scottish families settled in Northern Ireland. Keeping to themselves, they discouraged marriage to the local Irish citizens and became known as Scotch-Irish. Following the Irish famine of 1740 and 1741, it is estimated that over twelve thousand people a year fled to America. Richard Nimocks, born in 1744, in either Ireland or Scotland, married Zerviah Noble on December 15, 1772. Together they had at least ten children, including Fanny born on March 13, 1773; Noble on September 30, 1774; Electra on April 4, 1778; Roland on May 18, 1780; Zerviah on September 10, 1782; Nancy on September 10, 1784; Jared on October 4, 1786; Oliver on August 11, 1788; Walter on June 15, 1792; and Lucy on January 15, 1795. According to family legend, Richard came to America from the Scottish highlands or northern Ireland with his parents and his brother James around 1746. Their parents died on the voyage, leaving the boys to be raised by strangers, most likely from the Westfield area. Richard purchased land in Westfield in 1769, at the age of twenty-five. While serving in the War of Independence, Richard ordered a bounty coat from the camp at Roxbury. When Hessian prisoners of war were marched through Westfield on their way to Boston, Richard was one of the citizens who provided overnight shelter to the men. The next day, his nightcap was missing, never to be seen again.

Ezra Clapp, born to Preserved and Mehitable (Warner) Clapp on May 20, 1716, married Margaret Ingersoll on

October 13, 1743. Together they had at least six children including Molly born in July 1745, Margaret on August 10, 1747; Paul on June 19, 1748; Lydia on July 23, 1757; Ezra on May 24, 1760; and Charlotte on January 10, 1763.

From the will of George Phelps:

> The last Wil & Testamt of George Phelps of Westfield . . . who being cracy of Body though yet my Memory of understanding by God's Goodness is continued. . . . Concerning my Dear wife, I exhort my children to be careful & tender of her . . . that she want nothing that may be necessary to her comfortable subsistence, to hearken & attend to her Counsel from time to time. . . . I give to my son Jacob, four acres of the northerly end of my home lot here in my West field, with the house, barns & orchard upon it, only reserving one end of the house for my wife whilst she lives; and seeing he hath all my buildings here, he shall help his brothers John & Nathaniel. . . . I give to my son Isaac, the best coats of my apparel, & my Mare, the colt I give to his son Isaac my grand child . . . if anything appeare dubious . . . I order it be referred to the hearing & determination of our Reverend Pastor Mr. Taylor and Ensign Lumes.

Many families in the wilderness married their relatives. Aaron Phelps married his cousin Rachel Bagg on June 26, 1729, when Rachel was twenty-seven years old. They grew up next to each other, with Rachel's mother being Aaron's father's sister. Aaron and Rachel's daughter, Ruth, married her nephew Joseph Dewey, the son of her sister Hannah and brother-in-law Joseph.

Isaac Phelps, after moving to Westfield, became the town clerk, assessor, surveyor, town treasurer, and schoolmaster.

He was one of the foundation men of the church in 1679, being a substantial landowner on Main Street. On August 17, 1684, a jury consisting of John Maudesly, John Root, Samuel Root, Samuel Loomis Sr., John Sacket, Jacob Phelps, Isaac Phelps, John Ponder, John Williams, Thomas Noble, Josiah Dewey, and Thomas Dewey, delivered their "judgmt on the awful, amazing and untimely death of Eleezer Weller, after due notice taken, we all unanimously agree, that through the strength of temptation he became his own executioner, by hanging himself, all signs and circumstances freely concurring therein, and nothing appearing to the contrary, to the best of our judgments, we suppose he might be dead twenty four hours before it was known."

Eleezer Weller was married to the widow Mary Phelps by John Holiak (Holyoke) on November 1, 1704. Together they had at least six children, including Jonathan born on September 3, 1705; Mary on February 26, 1707; Margaret on September 26, 1709; Nathaniell on October 18, 1710; David on October 14, 1713; and Ebenezer on October 16, 1713. David and Ebenezer were twins born forty-eight hours apart. Mary drowned in April of 1753, being swept off her horse while crossing the Great River at King's Meadow with Mary Kellogg. On December 20, 1757, Ebenezer's three year old son died, scalded by a skillet of hot milk.

Nathaniel Weller married Deliverance Hanchett, daughter of Deacon Thomas Hanchett. Her sister Hannah married Samuel Loomis of Westfield. Deacon Hanchett moved to Westfield in 1670, living on Elm Street. He later moved to Suffield, Connecticut, where he was "freed from trayning considering his age and crazyness," on September 25, 1683. Nathaniel and Deliverance received the deacon's Westfield orchard as part of his estate when he died in 1686. The Wellers lived on the corner of Court and Elm Street and had two daughters, Thankful and Sarah. Nathaniel was a selectman, and was elected to be the second deacon of the church in 1692.

The solution for legal recourse in the new town was established in 1671, when Joseph Whiting, George Phelps and Aaron Cook were "allowed to be commissioners to end small causes at Westfield, (not exceeding 40 shillings value.)" In December of 1672, it was "voted that the town will go on with building a meeting house with all convenient speed as may be. The dimensions are as follows 36 foots square and the form to be like Hatfield meeting house. . . . Mr. Joseph Whiting, Deacon Hanchett, John Sacket, John Root, & Aaron Cook are chosen to manage all concerns about it for the best advantage to the town." It was constructed on the north side of Main Street.

John Root, born on July 10, 1646, in Farmington, Connecticut, was married to Mary Ashley in Springfield by the Reverend Fayette Chapin on October 18, 1664, settling on the fort side in Westfield with his brothers Samuel and Thomas. Together John and Mary had at least nine children, including Mary born on September 22, 1667; Joshua in 1669, Sarah on September 14, 1670; John on December 18, 1671; Samuel on September 16, 1675; Hannah on December 9, 1677; Abigail on June 26, 1680; Joshua on November 23, 1682; and Mercy on January 15, 1685. In 1669 he was made a freeman, and in September, John became the first town clerk of Westfield. When the drums first beat the call to worship in the new First Church on August 27, 1679, John was one of the seven foundation members. He was town clerk from 1716 to 1730, a Lieutenant in the militia, and elected selectman eleven times. President Rutherford B. Hayes, Bess Truman, and Clint Eastwood can all claim John Root as their ancestor.

Deacon Joseph Root Junior, born to Ensign Joseph and Sarah on August 23, 1715, became a deacon in 1769. He married Ann Bancroft on September 8, 1743, and together they had at least six children including Desiar born on August 10, 1744; Silas on September 20, 1747; Joseph on August 28, 1749; Desiar on July 21, 1753; Abner on October 4, 1757; and Silas on March 31, 1759.

Deacon John Shepard, born to William and Experience (Hart) Shepard in 1673 in England, married Elizabeth Woodruff on December 21, 1703, in Westfield. Together they had at least seven children, including Jonathan on September 27, 1704; John on November 18, 1706; Ezekiel on November 23, 1709; Elizabeth on February 14, 1712; Sarah on April 21, 1715; David on January 22, 1718; and Mary on June 15, 1725. John bought land in Westfield from John Fowler on July 29, 1696, and received about ten acres to settle grants made to his grandfather Hart. He stated his occupation as tanner, and married his second wife, Abigail Sackett, widow of David King, on May 24, 1733. Abigail, Ezekiel, David, and Mary all died of consumption within a month's time in the summer of 1743.

Deacon Gideon Shepard served in the Baptist Church of Westfield, and was a sergeant in Lieutenant John Shepard's company of minutemen in the 1775 march to Lexington. In the fall of 1777, he served as sergeant in Captain Mosely's company in the march to Saratoga, New York. Born on January 6, 1747, to Deacon John and Elizabeth (Noble) Shepard, he married Silence Noble on November 13, 1766. Together they had at least seven children, including Silence born on June 2, 1767; Gideon on May 15, 1769; Winthrop on June 20, 1772; Pelatiah on December 15, 1774; Eli on April 7, 1777; Sophia on January 26, 1779; and Roxana on February 4, 1781. Deacon Gideon died on December 28, 1790, of consumption at age forty-three. When his mother, Elizabeth, died on November 12, 1793, she had one hundred and eighty descendants, twenty-seven of whom predeceased her.

Reverend Edward Taylor married Elizabeth Fitch on January 2, 1674. Together they had at least eight children, including Samuel; Elizabeth on December 27, 1676; James on October 12, 1678; Abigail on August 6, 1681; Bathshua on January 1683; Elizabeth on February 5, 1685; Mary on July 3, 1686; and Hezekiah on February 18, 1688. On June 2, 1692, Taylor married Ruth Willis, granddaughter of Connecticut Governor George Wyllys, and together they had at least six children, including Ruth born on April 16, 1693; Naomi on March 30, 1695; Ann on July 7, 1697; Mehitable on August 14, 1699; Keziah on April 4, 1702; and Eldad on April 10, 1708. Reverend Taylor is now considered to be one of America's first poets, but true to his wishes, the public was unaware of his gift for verse until a collection of his works was published in 1939 by Yale. The school had received the works from Taylor's heirs in 1883. Many of his poems were written as spiritual exercises prior to preparing for communion services. He was described by his contemporaries as being small in stature, with intense charm and a strong personality. Unable to afford the cost of many books, Taylor became adept at copying his favorite books in longhand, leaving over two hundred volumes in his estate.

Reverend Dr. Ezra Stiles, grandson of Reverend Edward Taylor and president of Yale College from 1778 thru 1795, was known for speaking his mind. "The business of one half of the town is to sell rum, and the other half to drink it."

Eldad Taylor served in the first state "Continental" congress in Boston. He wrote back to his wife in Westfield when the British evacuated Boston on March 18, 1776:

> "My Dear: This morning opens with much news . . . The Ministerial Vermin left Boston yesterday morning in ye utmost confusion . . . ye tories about a fortnet ago was in high spirits encouraging ye troops that they should be soon masters of America but--when orders were given to prepare to sail, they were struck with paleness & astonishment. . . . Mortifying indeed."

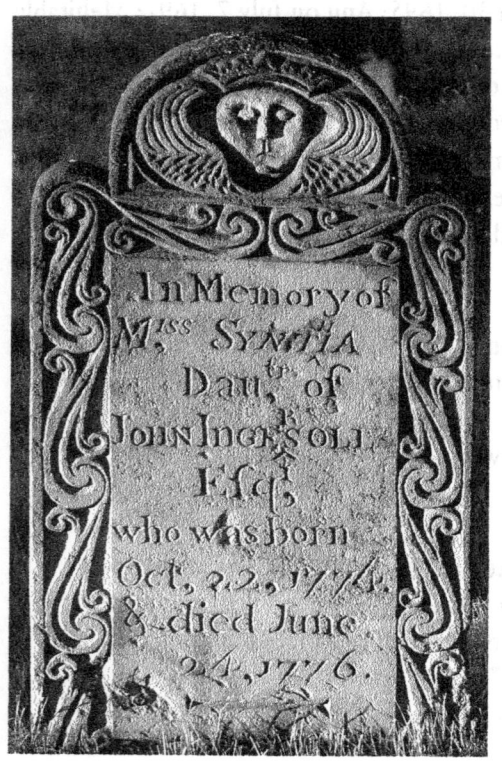

In Memory of
Miss Synthia
Dautr of
John Ingersoll
Esq'r
who was born
Oct 22, 1774
& died June
24, 1776

Carved by Stebbins shop

Rev Noah Atwater
the 4th Minister of the
Congregational Church in
Westfield, after a ministry of
20 years died Jan 25th 1802
aged 50

Mrs Rachel Atwater
Died Sep 16, 1787
in her 35 year

Mrs Anna Atwater
Died Aug 28, 1824 aged 70

In vain were life, if saints were ne'er to die
Life is their warfare, death their victory

In Memory of
Mr Samuel
Kellogg
who died May
27th 1761 in his
75 Year

A law eternal
does decree
that all things born
shall mortal be

Carved by Joseph Williston

*In Memory of the
Rev John
Ballantine
late Pastor of the
Church of Christ in
this place, who died
Feb 12, 1776 in the
60 Year of his age &
ye 35 of his Ministry*

*Mark the perfect Man
& Behold the upright
for the end of that man
is Peace*

Carved by Stebbins shop

The Reverend John Ballantine, born on October 30, 1716, to John and Mary (Winthrop) of Boston, married Mary Molly Gay on July 20, 1743. Together they had at least eight children including Mary born on December 10, 1744; Lydia on April 20, 1747; John, who was ordained as a pastor but never married or preached, on April 18, 1750; William on July 11, 1751; Winthrop born on March 16, 1754 and died on September 23, 1758; Ebenezer on July 14, 1756; Lydia on March 16, 1759; and Winthrop on June 9, 1762. He preached in Providence, Rhode Island, in January of 1740, while their existing preacher recovered from a broken leg. On January 30th of that year, he was in Smithfield preaching in a wigwam at an Indian woman's funeral service. He was a frequent guest preacher in Suffield, Connecticut over the span of his career.

The Reverend kept a journal, recording daily visits to local families, praying over the sick and infirm, as well as interesting observances. In the entry of November 18, 1755, Ballantine wrote, "An earthquake, little after 4, threw down bricks from the top of many Chimneys." In 1756, he broke down the twenty deaths in town by age: two stillborn, four infants before age two, one death between ages two and three, three between ages ten and twenty, one between ages twenty and thirty, one between ages thirty and forty, three between ages forty and fifty, three between ages fifty and sixty, one between ages sixty and seventy, and one between eighty and ninety. Three soldiers, Sergeant Connor of Newbury, Robert Willis of Wofford, and David Davis of Rumford, drowned in the Great River on May 14, 1756.

He recorded weather reports, like the one for March 1757, that included snow on the 10th, snow on the 24th and 25th, rain on the 26th and 27th, raw on the 28th and 29th, and hail on the 30th; and on October 27, 1765, he wrote, "snow in night, snow all day, winter weather, snow too moist, seven inches deep. Preached, few attended Public Worship."

On July 18, 1759, he described what appears to be a tornado:

> Barn destroyed by a Whirlwind the 10 Instant. Nothing remained of the house but a chimney, five or six feet high, an oven in another place, part of the lower floor. Did not see two pieces of timber that held together. The timber chiefly broke and shattered. The house not only blown down, but the material blown away. Large timbers thrown some rods from the house. . . . Not much of the materials in sight of the house. . . . Some Poles, blown from the fence, came down with such violence, that they stuck two feet in the ground. Nails in a cask stuck into trees, pulled out with fingers with some difficulty. Household furniture so scattered as little of it to be found. At eight miles distance a Negro man killed. The owner of the house much hurt, also a traveler. A child carried 40 rods from the house over tops of trees, the rest in the house being twelve in all, wonderfully preserved. Two horses killed. . . . See here is this dispensation, a display of the power of God. Who will not fear to offend Such a God. He is Lord of Hosts. Storms, Wind fulfill His word.

His writing became more introspective as he aged, when he wrote on November 10, 1759, "My Birth Day, 1716. I have lived 43 years in the world. Do I live as becomes one that has had so much time & many advantages to know my duty. How have I spent this time. Have I spent it for God, my Great Master, who I am so many accounts obliged to serve. How great has been God's patience toward me. I am nearer my end, and nearer to God, nearer to heaven. May I work while the day lasts, for the night comes wherein no man can work," and on January 25, 1765, "Visited John Jones' Wife, who last Monday night had a fit and fell into the Fire. No help there, was grievously burned, so there is but little hope of life. May my eyes affect my heart. If so terrible to lay a little while in the Fire, how terrible is it to depart into everlasting Fire."

The journal contains descriptions of penalties suffered by wrongdoers, as well, like the entry on June 20, 1760, "Two Vagabond Persons, a Man & his Wife, were whipped for Stealing. They called their name Cunningham," and on September 6, 1760, "One Neal, who calls himself a Doctor, has been in town about a month, was living with Dr. Smith, was publicly whipped for Stealing," and on March 17, 1761, "Was at Justice Taylor's. Ralph, Captain Mosely's Negro, examined by him for assaulting Mary Shepard the night before. Whipped twenty-eight stripes."

In his reflections, he showed himself to be a man of forward vision. On February 10, 1761, he visited Agawam and attended a lecture:

> "Mr. Lathrop [of West Springfield] began with prayers . . . Mr. Breck [of Springfield] preached, then I prayed. . . . It was a rare instance of Catholicism which I was well pleased with. It appears to me quite remarkable that we should have communion with those whom we hope to live with in heaven, though they differ from us in some non-essentials. . . . Should Christians deal with one another, perhaps God has left some things obscure to try Christians, to exercise their Charity. It is arrogance in any man to set himself as a standard & condemn or approve of persons as they conform or not conform to him. I disclaim Infallibilty myself & I won't allow it to any man. Be not called master. Call no man Master. Allow to others what you claim as your right as a man."

There were times when the local people meted out their own form of justice, as Reverend Ballantine wrote on October 21, 1761, "A number of Turkey Hills people in conjunction with people from the south part of this town, violently took Eldad Phelps' wife & set her on a rail & carried her on their shoulders, set her likewise on a sharp back horse, carried her along, howling at her & ringing cowbells, blowing horns. The pretense was illicit Commerce with Ephraim Noble & Mistreatment of her husband." With farming an essential ingredient of daily life, gardening information was included in his journal, like the entry for June 4, 1763, "Worms do great hurt to gardens. We put hen dung and ashes about Cabbages to preserve them. Boil Bascom Cabbage, alias Jerusalem weed, water them with liquor." Social indiscretions were a common topic of discussion, like the entry for July 1, 1764, in which, "Mehitable Taylor delivered. God delivers her from trouble, which her sins brought upon her. O the goodness of God, may it lead to her repentance. May our young ones flee youthful lusts."

In Memory
of Winthrop
Son of ye Revd
Mr John &
Mrs Mary
Ballantine
who died after
a short Illness on
Sept 23 1758 Aged
4 Years & 5 months

Carved by Joseph Williston

In Memory of
Mr Edward
Martindale
who died March
ye 21st 1763 in ye
74 Year of his
Age.

Remember death.

Carved by Aaron Bliss

This monument is erected
in memory of
Capt John Bancroft
who was born April 19, 1722
and died June 27th 1793
in the 72d year of his Age.
Also
Mrs Mercy Bancroft, wife of
Capt John Bancroft,
who was born May 16, 1729
and died Feb 21st 1779
in the 49th year of her age.

Some hearty Friend shall drop his
tear on our dry bones and say
These once were strong as mine appear
and mine must be as they
Thus shall our mouldring Members teach
What every one Should learn
For dust & Ashes loudest preach
men's infinite Concerns

In Memory of
Major Samuel Mather
son of Samuel Mather
Esqr & Mrs Grace Mather
who died March 15 1789
in ye 25 Year of his Age

Life is uncertain Death is sure
Sin is ye wound & Christ ye cure
How oft are we in early Age
by death took from this mortal stage
like flowers cut down when fresh and green
so we by death are no more seen

Carved by Stebbins shop

In Memory of
Mr Ebenezer
Bush Who died
November 10th 1757
in ye 71st year
of his age

Know then this truth
Enough for man to
know virtue alone
is happiness below

One of the many ways used to preserve ancient gravestones is to encase them in concrete slabs. This often results in further breakage to the stone.

Here Lies ye
Body of mrs
Mary ye wife
of mr Aaron
Bush who de-
Parted this
Life with A
Comfortab el
end march 28
1768 in ye 45
year of her age

Carved by Thomas Spelman

In Memory of
Mr Richard Nimocks
who died
23rd Augt 1803
Aged 59 Years

Turn here my chil
dren as you pass
& view my bed of clay
swift as the sand
spins from the glass
man's life doth pass away

Carved by John Ely

Memento Mori
[Remember Death]

In Memory of
Mr Ezra Clap
who died Octr 25th
AD 1768
In the 53rd Year
of his Age

All you that stand & view
this stone
Prepare for death as I
have done

Carved by Solomon Brewer

In Memory of
General
WARHAM PARKS
who died
March 6th 1801
Aged 49 Years

Also of Elizabeth
daughter of
General Warham and
Rebecca Parks who
died Feb 1st 1800
Aged 20 Months

Carved by John Ely

Warham Parks was born on March 13, 1752, to Elisha and Mary (Ingersoll). He graduated from Harvard in 1773, joined the Continental Army as a captain in 1775, leading Westfield's minutemen, and eventually attained the rank of brigadier general. Major Parks was wounded at the Battle of Saratoga on October 7, 1777. After the war he became a justice of the peace, and married his cousin Molly Ingersoll on January 4, 1778. Together they had at least three children including Julia born on August 20, 1778; Polly on October 9, 1781; and Elisha on June 8, 1790. He married Rebecca Gorham in Charlestown on December 20, 1791, and together they had at least six children including Gorham on May 5, 1794; Mary on August 30, 1795; Rebecca on August 6, 1796; twins Elizabeth and Rufus on May 24, 1798; and Elizabeth on December 19, 1800. Gorham Parks married Mary Ann Thompson of Waldboro, Maine, became a member of Congress, ran for governor of Maine, and served as the Minister to Brazil.

On March 5, 1778, General George Washington wrote to Major Warham Parks, "Colonel Shepard has communicated to me the contents of your letter to him on 24th November last. Your scruples relative to continuing in the Service from the motives you mention, are the suggestions of a generous mind. . . . Your absence till the Campaign opens will be of no essential detriment to the Corps you belong to; and both that and the Service had better dispense with your presence for a time than lose you altogether."

*Sacred to ye Memory
of Mrs Jerusha Phelps
wife of Mr John
Phelps who departed
this life Octr the 1st
AD 1769 in ye 29th
Year of her Age*

*Jesus saith unto her I am
the resurection and the
life he that believeth in me
though he were dead
yet shall he live*

Carved by Aaron Bliss

In Memory
of Mr
Jonathan
Weller
who died Augst
1st 1744 In
his 39th year

Carved by William Holland

Notice the unusual combination of a cherub on
the top and a winged skull on the bottom of this stone.

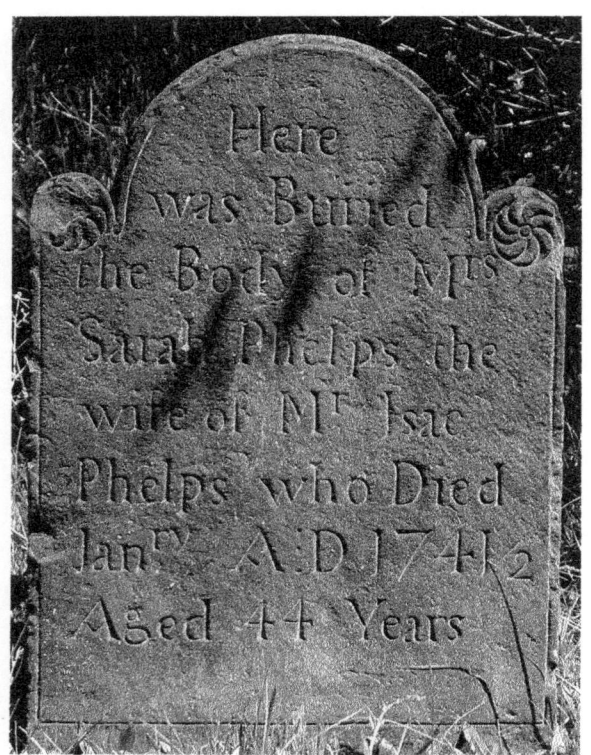

Here
was Buried
the Body of Mrs
Sarah Phelps the
wife of Mr Isac
Phelps who Died
Janry AD 1741/2
Aged 44 Years

Carved by Joseph Johnson

JOHN
ROOT AGED
ABOUT 44 YEARS
HE DYED THE 24TH
OF SEPT 1687

Carved by George Griswold

Hon William Shepard
died
Nov 16 1817
aged 80

He fought the battles of our Country
Aided in the councils of our nation
& exemplified the character of the Christian

The righteous shall be in
everlasting remembrance

General William Shepard, born on November 20, 1737, to Deacon John and Elizabeth (Noble) Shepard, married Sarah Dewey on January 31, 1760. Together they had at least nine children, including William II on March 19, 1760; Turner on September 16, 1762; Charles on September 27, 1764; Sarah on February 17, 1767; Noah on February 20, 1769; Nancy on October 25, 1771; Warham on December 26, 1773; Lucy on December 15, 1778; and Henry on June 24, 1782. William Shepard began his long and distinguished military career at age seventeen in the French and Indian War. By age nineteen, he was a sergeant during the Canadian Campaign, and in 1758 he was a lieutenant under General Abercrombie. The next year, he was a captain with General Amherst. After spending thirteen years as a private citizen in Westfield during an era of peace, he was commissioned a Lieutenant Colonel in Timothy Danielson's regiment in May of 1775, and by January of 1776, he was commanding the 3rd Continental Infantry. He served with General Horatio Gates, helping to defeat General Burgoyne at the battle of Saratoga in 1777.

Shepard was wounded while serving in New York covering the retreat from Long Island, taking a musket ball in the neck. While the surgeons were probing for the ball, he said, "Bring me a canteen." Discovering that he could drink and talk, he told the surgeon, "It is all right, doctor, stick on a plaster and tie on my cravat, for I am going out again." Against the advice of the attending surgeons, Shepard returned to battle, adding to his growing legend. General George Washington made Shepard his aide in the battle of Monmouth, spending the winter at Valley Forge. Following the Revolutionary War, he was elected to the governor's council for five years, and was a state representative for six years. On April 29, 1789, he was chosen to be a deacon of the First Congregational Church.

General Shepard was successful in leading the fight against the local Regulators in the attack on the federal armory in Springfield, while at the same time alienating many of his neighbors and friends in spite of his stellar record during the

war. His personal property was destroyed on numerous occasions by sympathizers to the rebellion.

The current Franklin Street in Westfield was home to the Shepard family since 1702, and was once called Shepards Lane, where General Washington visited his old comrade on his swing through New England. When the town meeting voted to change it to Franklin Street, many local residents were upset, stating that Benjamin Franklin had been honored all over the country, but Shepard was unlikely to be honored anywhere outside of Westfield.

In 1913, Henry Fuller bequeathed one hundred dollars to construct a monument to General Shepard. A committee consisting of J.C. Greenough, A.D. Robinson, William T. Smith, Henry W. Ely, and Arthur S. Kneil contracted Augustus Lukeman to create the monument, which was dedicated on September 3, 1919. There have been countless theories expressed as to why the statue of the general should be facing away from the common green in the center of town. In the late 1940s, the monument still retained its original bright copper color. It was found to contain very little copper content, being built during the first world war when copper was scarce, and in 1951 a special acid was applied to the monument, allowing the desired green hue of normal copper oxidation to gradually appear.

Here Rests ye Body
of ye Revd Mr Edward
Taylor ye Aged
Venerable learned
& Pious Pastor of ye
Church of Christ in
this Town who after
He had Served God
and his Generation
Faithfully for Many
Years fell asleep
June 24th 1729 in ye
87th year of his Age

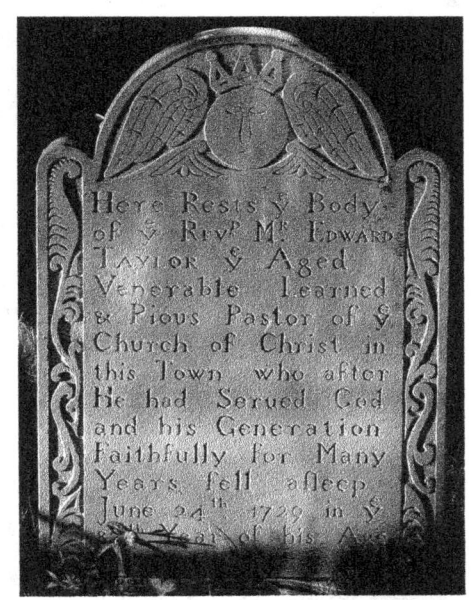

Original stands in church courtyard.

Reproduction carved in the 1970s.

ZENAS ATKINS
was suddenly kill'd while
riding in a sleigh and coming
in contact with another in turn-
ing a corner on the evening of
Jan 14, 1816
Aged 34

SOPHIA
his widow
died May 18 1846
Aged 65

In Memory of
Josiah Scovel
who died
Nov 26th 1821
aged 82 years
Also Fanny wife of
Josiah Scovel
who died
March 2d 1806
aged 72 years
She was buried in
Haddam Conn

Carved by Hermon Newell

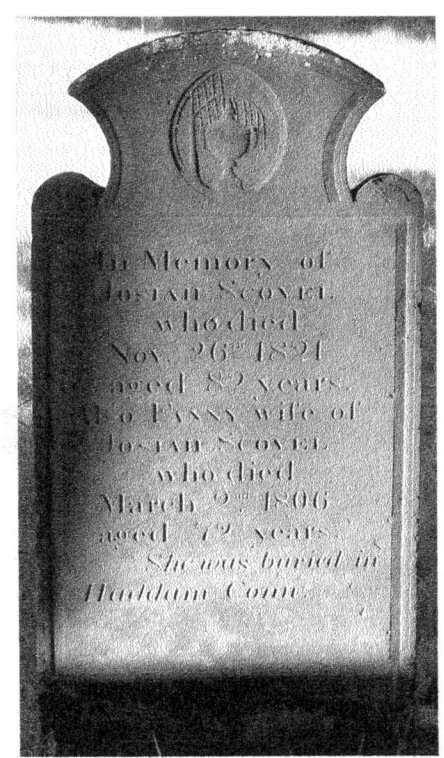

Mundale Burying Grounds

The first burying ground in the Mundale section is now located far from the main road, deep in the woods and away from prying eyes. Without local help in finding it, one can easily get lost and the graveyard is left to itself. It is said that the burying ground filled up, with no room left for more burials, but there are few remaining stones to mark the old graves. There were two options: one was to expand the current boundaries, and the other was to establish a new burying ground elsewhere. At the time, there was a growing split in the Mundale congregation. The Hot Water Party

believed an occasional strong drink would warm the body, driving out the cold of New England winters, and was led by Thomas Loomis, who preferred expanding the existing burying ground. The Cold Water Party, who believed it was healthier to restrict one's intake to cold water, was led by Lucas Cowles, who advocated opening a new graveyard, and donated some of his land for that purpose.

When construction began on Cobble Mountain Reservoir in Blandford, graves from the South Street Cemetery needed to be relocated. Austin Phelon of Granville obtained permission to move five family plots to Mundale Cemetery. Despite a thorough search, only three bodies were recovered, John Junior, Fally, and Mary. The remains of John and Mary Phelon, the original family settlers, were never found.

Lieutenant John Phelon, born on May 31, 1761, married Mary Lamb of Springfield. It was said that he cared more for money than religion. Together they had at least four children, including Hannah born on March 4, 1786; John on May 22, 1790; Gad on November 13, 1793; and Polly in 1797.

Rufus was born in 1778 in Granville to Nathaniel and Prudence (Root) Gillett, and married Tryphena Root on April 17, 1808. Together they had at least five children, including Henry born in 1810; Maria on November 12, 1811; Samuel on August 3, 1815; James on June 15, 1817; and Caroline on November 5, 1821.

Apollos, born to Lucas and Lydia (Noble) Cowles on May 26, 1835, married Caroline Pinckman on October 10, 1852. Together they had

Lucas, born in June of 1853. A few weeks later Caroline died, and Lucas died a month after his mother. Apollos then married Henrietta Maria Granger on October 23, 1861. Together they had Frederick on January 12, 1862.

In memory of
Lieut John Phelon
West Springfield May 31 1761
Blandford Dec 1821
and his wife Mary Lamb
Springfield Dec 1 1762
Granville Aug 14 1847
Erected by their great granddaughter
Ellen Lucy Phelon Barnes

In
Memory of
Harriet E Phelon
who fell asleep
Apr 17 1845
AE 19 Yrs

Them which sleep in Jesus will God
bring with him

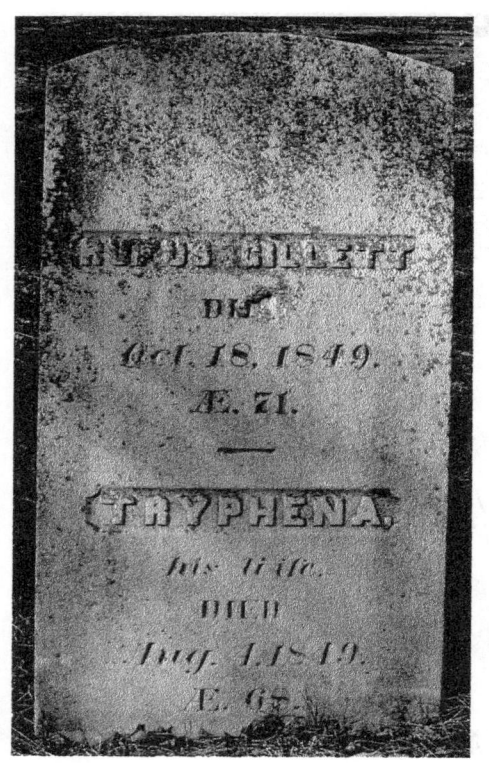

RUFUS GILLETT
Died
Oct 18 1849
AE 71

TRYPHENA
his wife
DIED
Aug 4, 1849
AE 68

CAROLINE A
wife of
Apollos Cowles
DIED
Aug 25, 1853
aged 26

APOLLOS COWLES
DIED
Aug 22 1862
aged 37

It is appointed unto man once to die
and after that the judgement
Friends nor Physicians cannot save
My mortal body from the grave
Nor can the grave confine me here
When Christ shall call me to appear

Middle Farms Cemetery

Solomon Root & Wife
Died 1790
Were of the first
settlers of
Westfield Farms
& Great Grand
Parents of
Capt Horace Root
of this town

The first recorded burial in the Middle Farms Cemetery was in 1790. Solomon Root and his wife, great-grandparents to Captain Horatio Root, were among the first settlers of the Middle Farms area of Westfield. Their descendants erected a monument for them many years after their deaths.

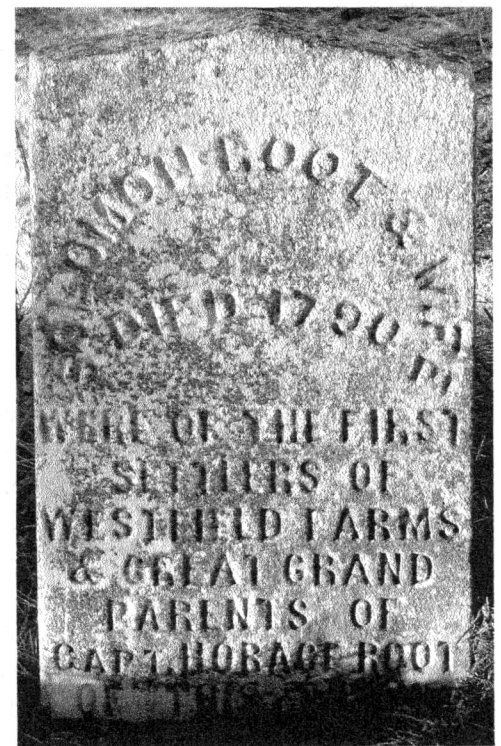

Reverend Samuel Buell, born on June 22, 1713, in Killingworth, Connecticut, married Lydia Wilcox on January 1, 1735. Together they had at least five children, including Jemima in 1735, Abigail in 1738, Lydia in 1740, Samuel on June 2, 1742; and Jerusha on November 5, 1749. In January of 1742, Samuel went to Northampton to preach during the Great Awakening, filling in for a traveling Reverend Jonathan Edwards. Jerusha married into American nobility when she wed David Gardiner of New York, a Yale graduate. His father's will of 1762 gives, "to my son, David Gardiner, my Island, lying near the east end of Long Island."

Lieutenant Samuel Buell, born on June 2, 1742, married Clarinda Hoadley in 1766. Together they had at least eight children, including Rowland in 1768, Benjamin in 1770, Bela in 1774, Lucy in 1776, John in 1781, Pitman in 1783, Samuel in 1785, and Lucy in 1787.

The Eglestones came from Windsor, Connecticut. Nathaniel, born on April 3, 1712, married Esther Waite of Northampton, and together they had at least six children including Nathaniel born in 1741, Esther in 1743, Editha in 1747, Dolly in 1749, Eber in 1751, and Abner in 1754. Eber Eggleston, born on June 13, 1751, married Submit Judd on September 21, 1777. Together they had at least ten children, including Eunice born in 1778, Eli in 1781, Eli in 1784, Submit in 1786, Eber in 1788, Eber in 1790, Judd in 1792, Laura in 1794, Esther in 1807, and Olive in 1800.

John Topliff moved to the West Farms locale around 1784, from Connecticut. Born on March 28, 1755, he married Susanna Jacobs, and together they had at least six children, including John in 1784, Stephen in 1789, twins Mary and Margaret in 1793, Nancy Ann in 1797, and Alfred in 1799.

ENOCH ROOT
DIED
Nov 17 1837
AE 64

LUCY
His wife died
July 17 1870
AE 94

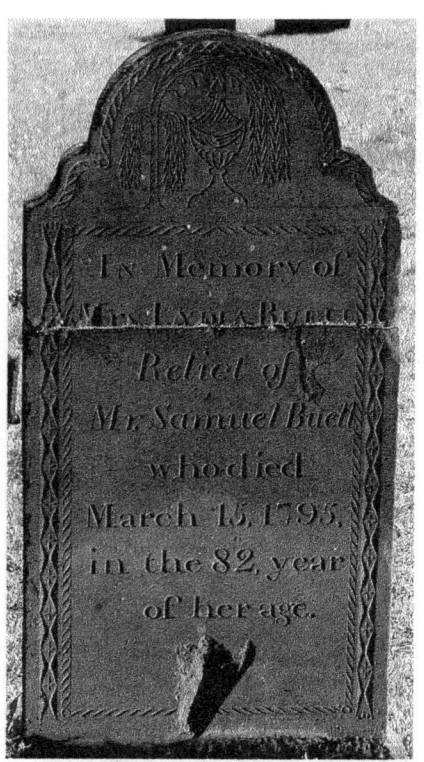

In Memory of
Mrs Lydia Buell
Relict of
Mr Samuel Buell
who died
March 15 1795
in the 82 year
of her age

SAMUEL BUELL
died
Sept 14 1819
AE 77 Ys

CLARENDA
wife of
Samuel Buell
died
June 16 1833
AE 93 Ys

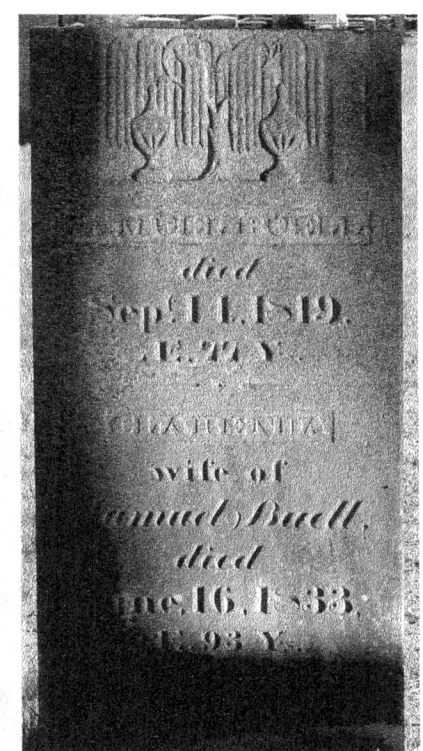

In Memory of
Mr Nath Eglestone
who Died March 7th
AD 1790
in the 78th Year
of his age
Time how short
Eternity how long

Footstone

EBER EGLESTON
died
Dec 25, 1815
AE 64 Ys
SUBMIT
wife of
Eber Egleston
died July 4 1821
AE 66 Ys
EUNICE
daughter of
Eber & Submit Egleston
died Aug 10 1803
AE 25 Ys

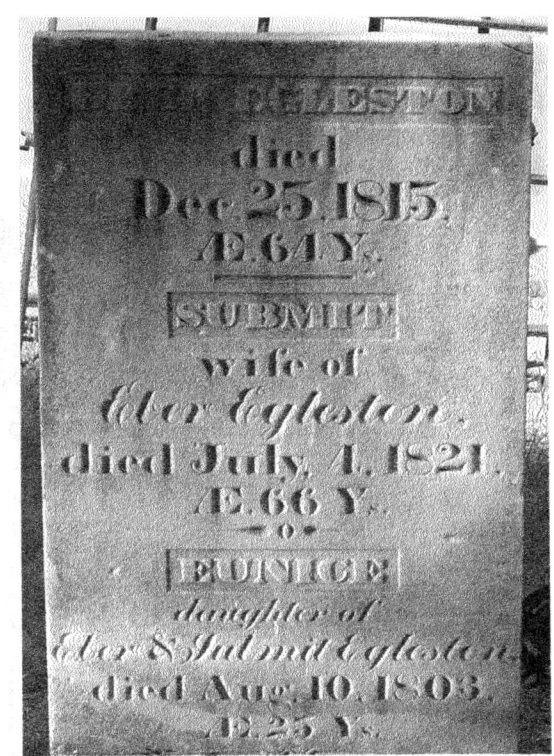

In Memory of
Miss Mary
Daughter of
Mr John & Mrs
Susanna Topliff
who died
17th Octr 1806
Aged 12 Years

Carved by John Ely

In Memory of
Capt Roswell
Clark
who died
10th Febr 1802
in the 40th Year
of his Age

Carved by John Ely

Pine Hill Cemetery

Zinc Civil War monument sponsored by the GAR

Pine Hill Cemetery was created in 1842. The numerous zinc monuments found here were an interesting sales gimmick of the late 1800s and early 1900s. Cunningly marketed as white bronze, and more affordable than true bronze, zinc markers were sold by travelling salesmen and each monument was made-to-order. A sales catalog displayed a wide array of structural elements to be mixed and matched; removable inscription panels could be easily replaced with a new epitaph as needed. These segments were manufactured by the Monumental Bronze Company of Bridgeport, Connecticut. They were in the monument business up until the beginning of World War I, when their plants were refurbished for munitions for the war effort. Many of the military statues and family monuments of the time were white bronze, and have withstood the elements of time and weather.

The Vadakin family chose a classic stone monument style for their zinc memorial.

The Bowen family explored the creative possibilities offered by zinc monuments.

Midshipman
Gilbert Fowler
U.S. Navy
Born at Westfield, Mass.
May 1st 1854
Died on board the
U.S. Flagship Franklin
Spezia, Italy
Aug 22nd 1874

Stone slabs placed over graves were called "wolf stones" and functioned as a device to protect those graves from molestation by animals, and later body-snatchers. These four large stones mark the final resting places of members of the Fowler family.

Owens District Cemetery

Abijah Owen lived on the west side of East Mountain Road, just past the sawmill on the bend in the road. Carmi lived in the next house on the same side of the road. Hiram Owen lived on the east side of Timber Swamp Road, just across the brook from Roswell Clark. Aaron Sibley lived on the north side of the street just past Holyoke Road.

Abijah, son of Asahel and Deborah (Drake) Owen, born on April 9, 1754, married Miriam Brooks in 1776. Together they had at least four children, including Emily in 1785, Abijah Jr. born on July 4, 1790; Rachel on October 9, 1796; and Charlotte.

Carmi, son of Asahel and Deborah (Drake) Owen, born on December 9, 1755, married Sarah Lindsay on August 26, 1781. Together they had at least ten children, including Carmi born in 1781, Sarah in 1782, Eunice in 1784, Phineas in 1786, Roswell in 1791, Elijah in 1794, Belinda in 1796, Lucinda in 1798, Julius in 1805, and Pliny in 1807.

Aaron Sibley married Triphena Agard, and together they had at least two children, including Mareett born in 1820, and Lucy Sibley born in 1823.

In Memory of
Mr Abijah Owen
who died
16th Novr 1808
in the 55th Year
of his Age

A husband kind
and parent dear
lies buried here

Carved by John Ely

C O
In
Memory of
Carmi Owen
DIED
July 16 1838
AE 83 Y's

In Memory of
Mrs Emily Owen
Daughter of Mr
Abijah & Mrs
Miriam Owen
who died
29th Octr 1808
Aged 23 Years
who is the first
in the yard

Carved by John Ely

AARON SIBLEY
DIED
Apr 25 1859
aged 79

Huswifery by Reverend Edward Taylor

Make me, O Lord, thy Spining Wheele compleate.
Thy Holy Worde my Distaff make for mee.
Make mine Affections thy Swift Flyers neate
And make my Soule thy holy Spoole to bee.
My Conversation make to be thy Reele
And reele the yarn thereon spun of thy Wheele.

Make me thy Loome then, knit therein this Twine:
And make thy Holy Spirit, Lord, winde quills:
Then weave the Web thyselfe. The yarn is fine.
Thine Ordinances make my Fulling Mills.
Then dy the same in Heavenly Colours Choice,
All pinkt with Varnisht Flowers of Paradise.

Then cloath therewith mine Understanding, Will,
Affections, Judgment, Conscience, Memory
My Words, and Actions, that their shine may fill
My wayes with glory and thee glorify.
Then mine apparell shall display before yee

The End

Glossary

Aetatis - Latin for "Of his or her age."

Cherub - winged head, see "Effigy"

Consort - husband or wife

Death's Head - skull, sometimes winged

Effigy - representation of "soul" or spirit

Efflorescence - growth of salt crystals on a surface caused by evaporation

Epitaph - inscription placed "over the grave"

Flexed Burial - human burial in semi-fetal position

Footstone - stone marker placed at the foot of the grave

Headstone - stone marker placed at the head of a grave

Ligature - character or letter combination of two or more letters

Long S - archaic form of the letter "s"

Marble - metamorphosed limestone

Mausoleum - above-ground tomb

Meeting House - building used for public meetings and religious services

Mourning Picture - lithographic or handcrafted remembrance, a memorial

Obelisk - four-sided monolith - tapering to a point

Obiit - properly mortem obiit, literally 'met death'

Pedestal - support for obelisk or tablestone

Portrait Stones - realistic representation of deceased on gravestone

Potters Field - burial place of poor and unknown

Probate Records - estate papers including wills and debts

Quarry - pit from which stone is obtained by digging, cutting, or blasting

Relict (also Relect) - widow

Sandstone - sedimentary rock composed of compacted sand

Signature - A gravestone carver's identifying mark or name

Spalling - chipping, flaking or crumbling of a gravestone

Sugaring - the "melting" of marble by acid precipitation

Tablestone - slab gravestone resting horizontally on legs or pedestals

Thorn - a character representing the sound "th"

Tympanum - semicircular area enclosed by an arch - also called a "lunette"

Viz - namely

Willow and Urn - mourning symbols of 1800s

The Last Word:

Thank you to Chris Lindquist and all of the research assistants at the Westfield Athenaeum, but especially to Joyce E. Peregrin and Jan Gryszkiewicz for getting just what I needed, just when I needed it.

Thank you to Dennis Picard for believing in us from the beginning, and offering input from his abundant knowledge along the way.

Thank you to Bob Plasse and the Westfield on Weekends organization for their support and belief in this project.

Thank you to Michele Plourde-Barker for her generous assistance and permission to use her research, which led to the addition of Mechanic Street Cemetery to the National Register of Historic Places.

Thank you to Bob Brown for retrieving treasures for use in this book during a hectic time.

Thank you to Bob Dewey for giving up a weekend to lead us on a tour of the Old Burying Ground.

Thank you to Nate Sperry and Steve Rheaume for taking the time to help a stranger find the old Mundale Burying Ground in the middle of nowhere.

Rusty is my other half, together we're more than complete. She built the foundation upon which this series is based. Her foresight and perseverance is an inspiration to us all.

Suggested Reading and Resources

Gravestone & Cemetery Books:
Enfield Connecticut, Stories Carved in Stone by Bob Clark, Dog Pond Press, 2006
Holyoke Massachusetts, Stories Carved in Stone by Rusty Clark, Dog Pond Press, 2006
Agawam Massachusetts, Stories Carved in Stone by Rusty Clark, Dog Pond Press, 2005
West Springfield Massachusetts, Stories Carved in Stone by Rusty Clark, Dog Pond Press, 2004
Gravestones of Early New England and the Men Who Made Them by Harriette Merrifield Forbes, Houghton Mifflin, 1927, 1966, 1989
Gravestone Chronicles I and II by Theodore Chase and Laurel Gabel, New England Historic Genealogical Society, 1997
Markers VIII, Association for Gravestone Studies, 1991
Markers XI, Association for Gravestone Studies, 1994
Graven Images: New England Stonecarving and Its Symbols, 1650-1815 by Allan I. Ludwig, Wesleyan University Press, 1966
Early New England Gravestone Rubbings by Edmund Gillon, Dover Publications, Inc., 1966

Buy Gravestone and Cemetery Books Online:
Association for Gravestone Studies:
http://www.gravestonestudies.org/store/books.htm
New England Historic Genealogical Society:
http://www.nehgs.org/store/main/

Local History:
Westfield Massachusetts 1669-1969 The First Three Hundred Years, edited by Edward C. Janes and Roscoe S. Scott, 1968
Historical Sketch of Westfield, Rev. Dr. Emerson Davis, 1852
An Authentic History of Westfield, Lewis M. Dewey, 1902

Electronic Media - CDs:
Vital Records of Springfield Mass to 1850 by Clifford L. Stott, NEHGS
The Corbin Collection Volume I, Hampshire County, Edited by Robert J. Dunkle, NEHGS
The Corbin Collection Volume II, Hampden County, Edited by Robert J. Dunkle, NEHGS

Online Sources for Gravestone / Historical Research:
The Farber Gravestone Collection:
http://www.davidrumsey.com/farber/
Connecticut Gravestone Network:
http://www.ctgravestones.com/
Symbolism on Old Gravestones - Guidelines for Gravestone Rubbings:
http://www.gravestonestudies.org/faq.htm
Connecticut Valley Historical Museum:
http://www.quadrangle.org/CVHM.htm

Old Deerfield, Massachusetts:
http://memorialhall.mass.edu/collection/index.html
http://deerfield-ma.org/museum.htm
http://www.historic-deerfield.org
http://1704.deerfield.history.museum/

Digital History - Primary Sources:
http://www.digitalhistory.uh.edu/
The History Place:
http://www.historyplace.com/index.html
Cornell University Library - Making of America:
http://cdl.library.cornell.edu/moa/
Library of Congress, American Memory:
http://memory.loc.gov/
Eyewitness to History:
http://eyewitnesstohistory.com/

Rootsweb - Surname Research:
http://worldconnect.rootsweb.com/cgi-bin/igm.cgi
History of Springfield I & II by Henry M. Burt 1898:
http://www.usgennet.org/usa/ma/county/hampden/
A Genealogical Dictionary of the First Settlers of New England Before 1692 by James Savage:
http://www.usgennet.org/usa/topic/newengland/savage/
Great resource for maps - 1500 to present day:
http://memory.loc.gov/ammem/gmdhtml/gmdhome.html
Old Photos/Postcards:
http://digitalgallery.nypl.org/nypldigital/index.cfm

Index

A

B

C

N

Q

Westfield Massachusetts - Stories Carved in Stone

Please send _____ copies of **Westfield Massachusetts: Stories Carved in Stone** @ **$15.95** each

Please send _____ copies of **Enfield Connecticut: Stories Carved in Stone** @ **$17.95** each

Please send _____ copies of **Holyoke Massachusetts: Stories Carved in Stone** @ **$15.95** each

Please send _____ copies of **Agawam Massachusetts: Stories Carved in Stone** @ **$13.95** each

Please send _____ copies of **West Springfield Massachusetts: Stories Carved in Stone** @ **$13.95** each

Shipping and Handling: $4.95 for one book $1.95 for each additional book (shipped to the same address)

My check or money order for $_____ is enclosed.

Please charge my:

Visa   MasterCard   AmericanExpress   Discover

Make check or money order payable to and send to:

Dog Pond Press
c/o eBizOpz
P.O. Box 27
West Springfield, MA 01090

Name _____

Address _____

City _____

State _____ Zip Code _____

Phone _____ E-Mail _____

Credit Card # _____

Exp Date _____ Signature _____

Payment must accompany order. Please allow 4-6 weeks for delivery.

*Please note that Dog Pond Press is a division of eBizOpz.
The charge for your book will show as a charge from eBizOpz on your next credit card statement.